WHY DID CHRIST DIE?

WHY DID CHRIST DIE?

F. E. Marsh

KREGEL PUBLICATIONS
Grand Rapids, Michigan 49501

Library of Congress Cataloging-in-Publication Data

Marsh, F.E. (Frederick Edward), 1858-1919.
  Why Did Christ Die?

  Reprint. Originally published: London:
Marshall Bros., c1921.
  1. Atonement. 2. Jesus Christ—Priesthood.
I. Title.
BT265.M335 1985   232'.3   85-18093
ISBN 0-8254-3249-9

Printed in the United States of America

Contents

Publisher's Preface 7

Introduction 9

1. Why Did Christ Die? 11

2. Comprehensiveness of Christ's Atonement . . 29

3. The Meaning of Christ's Atonement . . . 49

4. The Scriptures and Christ's Atonement . . 66

5. God and Christ's Atonement 81

6. Sin and Christ's Atonement 91

7. Christ and His Atonement 100

8. The Holy Spirit and Christ's Atonement . .112

9. Satan and Christ's Atonement 126

10. Holiness and Christ's Atonement . . .132

11. Service and Christ's Atonement . . .149

12. The Glory and Christ's Atonement . . .169

13. Four Errors Regarding the Atonement . .190

Publisher's Preface

One of the cardinal doctrines of the Christian faith is the death of the Son of God, Jesus Christ. Why is this so? Why did Christ die? What did Christ say about His forthcoming death on behalf of sinful humanity? These and other pertinent questions are answered in this thoroughly Christ-centered and soundly-Scriptural exposition of the atonement.

F.E. Marsh's striking work is unforgettable and blessing filled. He gives a concise study of the scope, meaning, glory and message of the atonement together with a chapter on four errors, taught by some today, concerning this foundational truth. He also brings out many practical applications of the Savior's death for the life and service of the believer.

Without compromise, Dr. Marsh takes the Scriptural stand, stating without equivocation, that Christ crucified is the greatest theme of the universe; for it proclaims the greatest work ever performed by the greatest Person, and accomplishes the greatest possible purpose—the conversion of men and salvation of souls.

This classic volume will strengthen the faith of the believer as he more fully understands all that was involved in the death of the Son of God on the cross of Calvary, and it provides outlines that the pastor and teacher can use for scores of messages on the death of Christ.

Introduction

Christ crucified is the greatest theme in the universe, for it proclaims the greatest work ever performed by the greatest Person, and secures the greatest possible ends.

Will you listen to the concessions of a Unitarian on the great truth of Christ's atonement? Thomas Starr King, a Unitarian, said: "The doctrine of the vicarious atonement is embodied by the holiest memories, as it has been consecrated by the loftiest talent of Christendom. It fired the fierce eloquence of Tertullian in the early Church, and gushed in honied periods from the lips of Chrysostom; it enlisted the life-long zeal of Athanasius to keep it pure; the sublimity of it fired every power, and commanded all the resources of the mighty soul of Augustine; the learning of Jerome, and the energy of Ambrose were committed to its defence; it was the text for the subtle eye and analytic thought of Aquinas; it was the pillar of Luther's soul, toiling for man; it was shapen into intellectual proportions and systematic symmetry by the iron logic of Calvin; it inspired the beautiful humility of Fénélon; it fostered the devotion and self-sacrifice of Oberlin; flowed like molten metal into the rigid forms of Edward's intellect, and kindled the deep and steady rapture of Wesley's heart. All the great enterprises of Christian history have been born from the influence, immediate or remote, which the vicarious theory of redemption has exercised upon the mind and heart of humanity."

Preaching Christ's atoning sacrifice we shall find it will be—

(1) A Convincer of Sin, as seen on the Day of Pentecost (Acts ii. 36, 37).

(2) A Bringer of Blessing, as evidenced in the lame man and Peter's words (Acts iii. 13—19).

(3) A Means of Forgiveness, as Peter emphatically states (Acts v. 29—31).

(4) A Procurer of Joy, as witnessed in the result of the Eunuch's faith (Acts viii. 29—39).

(5) An Obtainer of the Spirit, as was made known to Cornelius and those in his house (Acts x. 39—44).

(6) A Medium of Justification, as Paul declared at Antioch (Acts xiii. 38, 39).

(7) An Imparter of Responsibility, as the Apostle intimates to the elders at Ephesus, when he charges them to care for Christ's purchased possession (Acts xx. 28).

1

Why Did Christ Die?

One of the finest things that Dr. Dale ever uttered was, " Christ did not come to preach the Gospel, but that there might be a Gospel to preach." But that is only half the truth, for He not only came that there might be a Gospel to preach, but He proclaimed the Gospel He came to make. It is an unwarranted and an unscriptural fallacy to say, as a prominent free churchman has done, " There is a significant omission from the teachings of Jesus of any definite doctrine of a substituted and expiatory sacrifice." Such a statement displays culpable ignorance of what Christ taught about His death. Dr. Denney has well said, " The last months of our Lord's life was a deliberate and thrice-repeated attempt to teach His disciples something about His death." Christ spoke of a " baptism " He must experience (Luke xii. 50), of a " lifting up " He would endure (John iii. 14), of a goal He must reach (Luke xiii. 33), of a suffering through which He must pass (Luke xxiv. 7), of an hour with Him which must strike (John xii. 27), of a laying down of life which He would give (John x. 11), of a fulfilment of Scripture which He would make (Luke xxiv. 44), of a cup which He must drink (John xviii. 11), of a blood-shedding He would pour (Luke xxii. 20), of a love He would manifest (John iii. 16), of a death He would die (John xii. 24, 25), of a vicarious act He would perform (Matt. xx. 28), of a gift He would bestow (John vi. 51), of a work He would accomplish (John xix. 30), of a remission He would secure (Matt. xxvi. 28), of a power He would communicate (John vii. 39), of a profit that He would ensure (the word " expedient " in John xvi. 7 should be " profitable "), of an outcome of eternal life He would

obtain (John iii. 15), of a consecration He would assume
(John xvii. 19), of a victory He would gain (John xii. 31, 32),
of an experience through which He would pass (John
xii. 24, 25), of a forgiveness He would give (Luke xxiv. 46, 47),
of a God Whom He would glorify (John xvii. 4).

These are but some of the forecasts which Christ taught
about His death. We shall ponder the principal ones, as
answering the question, " Why did Christ die ?"

According to the teaching of Christ, His death was—

> Divine in its Provision
> Essential in its Necessity
> Voluntary in its Giving
> Substitutionary in its Offering
> Sufficient in its Atonement
> Complete in its Issue
> Practical in its Outcome

I. Christ taught that His death was *Divine in its Provision*.
There are two great and yet simple definitions of God,
namely, " God is Light " and " God is Love." Both of these
facts shine out at the Cross. " God is Light," and therefore
cannot pass over sin, nor allow it to go unpunished ; and
there shines out in letters of gold, too, at the Cross that
" God is Love," for He provides what He demands in the
sacrifice of Christ. Let us look at these two things in the
light of Calvary. " God is Light " and His claims must be
met in an expiation for sin, and that atonement was provided
by Himself, therefore, Christ's death was expiatory in its
sacrifice.

By expiatory in its offering we mean, that sin called for
punishment, that the sinner could not atone for his sin, and
that Christ has given to God a satisfaction for sin, that we
could never give ourselves.

Christ definitely teaches us the truth of expiation by sacrifice in His parable of the Pharisee and Publican, when He makes the latter repentantly cry, " God be propitiated to me, the sinner " (Luke xviii. 13, marg. R.V.), or " God make an atonement for me, the sinner." The word " Hilaskomai," rendered " be merciful " in the publican's prayer, is translated " make reconciliation for " in Heb. ii. 17, in referring to the high priest who " made an atonement " for the sins of the people on the Great Day of Atonement.

In the 16th of Leviticus the verb " Kaphar " occurs sixteen times, and is rendered " make an atonement " and " made a reconciling." From the verb " Kaphar " comes " Kopher," which is rendered " satisfaction " in Numbers xxxv. 32. What the publican recognised in his plea for mercy was the need of atonement or propitiation to be made for sin, for we may read his prayer in the light of the word used, and its translation in the other place, " God make reconciliation or expiation for my sin."

At once it will be apprehended the difference between the heathen thought of expiation and the Christian. With the heathen it is man's vain attempt to give satisfaction to the gods, but with the Christian it is what God stated long ago, " Deliver him from going down to the pit : I have found an atonement " (Job. xxxiii. 24, margin). God provides what He demands. This is the Gospel.

Canon Girdlestone in his Hebrew synonyms, in referring to the translations of the Hebrew and Greek words for atonement, says, " The prevailing idea set forth is the doing away with a charge against a person by means of expiation, propitiation, so that the accused may be received into the Divine favour, and be freed from the consequences of wrong-doing."

It will be clearly seen in the light of the Old Testament types, colouring as they do New Testament teaching, that

Christ endorsed the same in the prayer of the publican, and therefore taught that mercy is extended to the sinner because of His " Expiatory Sacrifice." In other words, God Himself, in the death of Christ, has provided satisfaction to Himself and obtained salvation for men ; as Dr. Dale truly said in speaking of Christ's atonement, " A propitiation for sin, originated and effected by God Himself, through which we are brought into such relations to God, that all moral reasons for withholding from us the remission of sins disappear. The death of Christ was a propitiation for the sins of men, because it was a revelation of the righteousness of God, on the ground of which He can remit the penalties of sin."

" God is Love." Christ taught that His death was the crowning act of God's manifested love. When Christ would tell us of God's love, He says, " For God so loved the world that He gave His only begotten Son." The same testimony is given in other portions of the New Testament. " God commendeth His love toward us, in that, while we were yet sinners Christ died for us." Mark what it says and does not say, it does not say, " Christ commendeth His love toward us," but " *God*." Again, " Herein is love, not that we loved God, but that He loved us, and sent His Son to be the Propitiation for our sins."

One of the noblest, among the many noble things during the war, was the sacrifice of a captain of one of the British patrol boats, who, after both legs had been shot off, ordered a fight against unequal odds to be continued, and commanded his men " to throw the confidential books overboard, and throw me after them." The captain's love of country prompted him to sacrifice life and limbs. That sacrifice came in the fortune and accident of war, but when God and Christ manifested their love for us, the former gave His Son and the latter laid down His life. Christ said,

" Greater love hath no man than this, that a man lay down his life for his friends " ; but herein is the wonder and the exceptional love of Christ, for He laid down His life for His enemies and sinners.

Everything about Christ on the Cross is a manifestation of love. If we look at the Cross we see *The Sacrifice of Love.* A truer word was never spoken when the crowd tauntingly said, " He saved others, Himself He cannot save." If He had saved Himself, He could not have saved others. At the Cross we hear *The Prayer of Love.* When His enemies treated Him cruelly, He prayed for them graciously, pleading with His Father to forgive them because they knew not what they did. We listen to *The Answer of Love* when, in response to the dying thief's prayer, " Lord, remember me," He replied, " To-day thou shalt be with me in Paradise." We behold *The Thoughtfulness of Love,* as He commits His mother to the care of the beloved John, and bids her to behold her son in him. We are moved by *The Anguish of Love* as the soul of Christ is torn by His inward sufferings and as He enters the throes of being forsaken by God. We see *The Thirst of Love* as He cries, " I thirst," and discover more than a request to have His thirst slaked, for He thirsted in soul agony that we might never cry for a drop of water in hell to cool our parched tongue. We see *The Victory of Love* as He reaches the goal of His purpose to die for our sins and to defeat the powers of hell in His exultant cry, " It is finished." We mark *The Committal of Love* as Christ dismisses His Spirit into the keeping of His Father. We look at *The Crown of Love* as we see the crown of thorns lacerating His sacred brow, for we know the thorns are symbolic of the curse He endured. We behold *The Work of Love* in Christ's transfixed hands, for there has never been anything so active in benefit as those passive hands of grace. We see *The Suffering of Love* in the pierced feet of our Lord, for the spikes which caused Him pain of body are emblematic of the iron that entereth into His soul. We behold *The Passiveness of Love* as Christ is stripped of His clothes and allows Himself to be crucified : He willed to suffer, for no will of man could have caused Him to suffer, and yet how potent and powerful is that death by which God is glorified and man is benefited.   We see *The Attractiveness of Love* in the magnetic force it had over the centurion, for he was impelled to confess, " Truly this man was the Son of God ; " and we see *The Heart of Love* in His pierced side, for that opened side expresses the open heart of God's love for us.

II. Christ taught that His death was *essential in its necessity*.   He said, " The Son of Man must be lifted up," and lest there should be any mistake we are informed that the lifting up had a significance of its own, " signifying what death He should die " (John iii. 14 ; xii. 32, 33), and of that death He said it " must be."   " Must " must mean " must," as Bengal says, " For this purpose He came down from heaven."   Some twelve times He uses the word " dei," rendered " must," " ought " and " behoved," and in each instance He refers to a necessity resting upon Him.   Dr. Dale, in commenting upon the passage in John iii., says : " His incarnation is not enough, His ministry is not enough . . . it is in this conception of His death that gives form to the words which follow," " For God so loved the world, that He gave "—did not merely send, but gave—" His only begotten Son "—surrendered Him up to all that was involved in the great work of saving mankind, delivered Him over to the death which has just been illustrated by a lifting up of the brazen serpent."

The late Professor Charteis made a similar statement : " There was only one Christian life that began at Bethlehem and ended at Calvary, every other Christian life begins at Calvary and goes back to Bethlehem."

The denial of the fact of sin is the cause of the denial of the necessity of Christ's atonement for sin. Recognise the fact and there is no questioning about the necessity of His death. No one who has ever felt the plague of his own heart will doubt the necessity of Christ's atoning death ; and, again, the sharp pinch of an accusing conscience and a sense of inability to rise to man's own ideals, leaving out God's requirement, will press a man to acknowledge the necessity of Christ's atonement, for as one has said, " The question of man's inability to any spiritual good accompanying salvation is a question as to matter of fact, and is to be answered ultimately by an appeal to experience. When a man has been discovered, who has been able, *without Christ*, to reconcile himself to God, and to obtain dominion over sin and over the world, *then* the doctrine of inability, or of the bondage due to sin, may be denied ; *then*, but *not till then*. If Christ is invariably needed to bring sinful man to the Father, and to give them that peace with God in which all spiritual achievements have their root, then man, so far as experience goes, has been completely disabled by sin ; and though he may have the right to boast among his equals, in his dealing with God boasting is excluded."

This inability in man, consequent upon his sin and sins, is scripturally demonstrated if we remember what God says man cannot do. " That which is crooked cannot be made straight " (Ecc. i. 15). The bend and trend of man's nature tends towards evil, like a wind-swept hedge, which leans the way the wind generally blows. " That which is wanting cannot be numbered " (Ecc. i. 15). Cyphers stand for nothing by themselves, so the sinner does not count, for he cannot pay his debt of obligation to God. " A good tree cannot bring forth evil fruit, neither can a corrupt tree bring forth good fruit " (Matt. vii. 18). Like produces like. A nettle

cannot be made into a rose tree, nor can man produce holiness
to the Lord since there dwelleth no good thing in him.
" Except a man be born again, he cannot see," or " enter the
kingdom of God " (John iii. 3-5). If a man is minus eyes and
legs, how can he see or walk ? Man's sin has blinded the
eyes of man's understanding and crippled the power of his
will, so that he cannot understand the things of God nor walk
in His ways. " A branch cannot bear fruit of itself " (John
xv. 4). A rootless branch is a fruitless one. So apart from
Christ man cannot bring forth fruit unto God. " They that
are in the flesh cannot please God " (Rom. viii. 8). They
may please themselves or others, but they cannot rise to the
plane of pleasing God. " Sacrifices " of ritual " can never
take away sins " (Heb. x. 11). Many think that acts of
religious observance will avail for the removal of their sins,
and gain acceptance with God, but He says that " can never "
be.

All this calls for someone apart from us, and beyond us, to
act for us. There is only one who can thus act, and that one
is Christ, who knowing the facts of the case, has stated the
necessity of His own death.

III. Christ taught that His death was *voluntary in its
Giving*. Five times in John x. Christ says He " giveth His
life for the sheep " (the word " giveth " is rendered " lay
down " in the other passages ; see John x. 11, 15, 17, 18).
The word " lay down " or " giveth " means to set, to place,
as the foundation for a house, as a candle in a stick, as a body
in a tomb, and as a purpose to be carried out. Christ's death
was no accident. He said He would lay it down of Himself,
and that no man had the power to take it from Him. His
star of destiny was His death on Calvary. The legendary
chasm, into which Marcus Curtius rode his horse at the
Forum of Rome, and caused what was a menace to close, is a

type of Christ's act of love as He faced our doom of sin and closed the hell of deserving for those who believe in Him.

As the man who brought a burnt offering brought it of " his own voluntary will " (Lev. i. 3), so Christ without any compulsion except the impulsion of His own love for us gave Himself for us.   Listen to what He says further.   " The Son of Man came to give His life a ransom for many " (Matt. xx. 28), so He summarizes the purpose of His coming into the world.   And again, He declares " The bread that I will give is My flesh " (John vi. 51).   And all through the New Testament we find the emphasis is on the fact that He " gave " Himself for us.   Does not all this tell us of His providing and pulsating love, and of His intense desire to bless us ?

IV. Christ taught that His death was *substitutionary in its offering*.   The Greek preposition " anti " is the one which expresses substitution, as all authorities are agreed.   It signifies one thing set over against another, or in place of another, as the anti-Christ, who is the usurper who takes the place of Christ ;   or " anti " is used to express an equivalent as the law recognised when it said, " An eye for an eye." " Anti " only occurs twice in connection with Christ's death directly.   Once in 1. Timothy ii. 6, and there it is part of another word, namely, " anti-lutron."   " Lutron " means a sum paid to loose something out of the market, and " anti " is instead of, therefore " anti-lutron " means a loosing price paid instead of others, for Christ is said to have " given Himself a ransom (anti-lutron) for all."   Christ practically used the same expression when He says, " The Son of Man came not to be ministered unto, but to give His life a ransom for (anti) many " (Matt. xx. 28).

A leading Free Churchman said sometime ago, " The remission of penalty, or the consequence of sin, does not depend upon the fact of Christ's death, but is obtained through the incorporation of His own life with the life of the human soul." This statement makes salvation depend, not upon the outside fact of Christ's acting in our place, and bearing our penalty, but partly upon Christ and partly upon man. In order that there may be no mistake as to his meaning, he further declares, " At eventide there will be light. Against that evening sky there is a Cross—see there are three crosses— God and humanity are suffering together. In this sense the forgiveness of sins is dependent upon redemption, because without that redemptive force working in us we could not feel true repentance."

If the author of these words had pondered the sacred words which fell from Christ's lips, instead of listening to the inner voice of his own thoughts, he would have found Christ never taught any such blasphemous doctrine as the sinful sufferings of sinful men being on a par with the sinless suffer- ing of the Divine substitute, nor suggest (if the words " blas- phemous doctrine " are too strong), the subjective experience of the believer is a procuring cause of salvation. To state such a thing is to get on what one describes, " The slippery slopes of subjectivity." Christ did not say He would give His life along with the lives of others for the remission of sins, but He did say His life was to be " a ransom for many," and the end He had in view was as He stated later, " for (or unto) the remission of sins " (Matt. xxvi. 28). " Remission " means not merely the remitting or cancelling of penalty, but the letting loose from the sins which brought the penalty, and that was one end He had in view in dying for us, in bearing the penalty instead of us. But it is one thing to speak of the result of Christ's death for us as a subjective power in separating us from sin and begetting within us true holiness ; and quite another to make that subjective experience to be a parallel basis of salvation. The objective reality of Christ's death as the vicarious offering for sin stands alone, and is alone the basis and procuring cause of salvation. Christ said it was " His blood " and not " His and ours " which was shed for the remission of sins. Christ made this so emphatically clear, that all four accounts of the Lord's Supper emphasise the fact that Christ would shed His blood for the remission of sins. Well does Dr. Dale exclaim, " The presentation of this central idea, notwithstanding the variations of the four narratives, is very impressive."

That " very impressive " fact, that Christ is alone in His atoning work, is further enunciated by the late Dr. Denney. He says, " The spirit in which Christ lived and died ought certainly to be our spirit ; we are to be identified with Him in His utter renunciation of evil, and in His complete devotion to God ; but no similar renunciation, no similar devotion on our part, even though they ended in literal crucifixion, could make our death identical in nature with that of the sinless One, Who, in dying, bore our sins. It is in this that the atonement lies. Christ finished it. He finished it alone. No one can do it after Him. No one needs to do it." Let us ponder these latter five sentences. " *It is in this that the atonement lies*," namely, that " in dying," He " bore our sins." This is what the Holy Spirit calls the Gospel, for Christ died for our sins, according to the Scriptures. There were sins to die for, and for our sins He has died. " *Christ finished it*." The Anointed One was sent to " accomplish " the work, and the work He has accomplished. " *He finished it alone*." He alone could do it, and He did it alone. " *No one can do it after Him*." There was no " after " to do, and there was no one who could do it if it were required. " There is no more offering for sin," since, through the once offered and only sacrifice the sins of the believer are remitted. *"No one needs to do it."* If there were the need, no man could meet it, and since there is no need what folly for any one to attempt it. Therefore we must come to this conclusion and no other, " It was *His* death, for He had *come* to die ; but it was *not* His, for He knew no sin ; it was *for us*, and *not for Himself*, that He made that death His own."

V. Christ taught that His death was *sufficient in its atonement*. Christ's own statement about His death is, " My flesh is meat indeed " (R.V.M., " True meat "), " and My blood is drink indeed " (R.V.M., " True drink ") (John vi. 55). Meat and drink are the material things which satisfy the hunger of the body. In like manner Christ's death and Christ Himself meets the hunger of the sin-conscious soul to its salvation and satisfaction, and also meets the claims of God to His satisfaction and delight. Many have wondered, as those did who heard Christ's words at the first, what He meant by eating and drinking His flesh and blood, but an explanation is found in the occasion under which Christ spoke the words, we are told, " The Passover, a feast of the Jews, was nigh." Doubtless the mind of Christ, while He refers to the manna, was filled with the Paschal Lamb, whose blood was shed and sprinkled on the doorstep and doorposts of the houses, and the flesh of the lamb, after roasting, was eaten by the Israelites. Christ is the Lamb of God's providing, and the Food of God's sufficiency ; and what Christ is insisting on is, as it was not sufficient for the blood to be shed and the flesh roasted, but the blood had to be applied and the flesh eaten, so Christ must be received and made one's own by faith. Ignatius expresses this in what he found Christ to be to him, when he says, " I have no delight in corruptible food, nor in the pleasures of this life. I desire the Bread of God, the heavenly bread, the Bread of Life, which is the flesh of Jesus Christ, the Son of God ; and I desire the drink of God,

namely, His blood, which is incorruptible love and eternal
life."

This provision is sufficient in a double sense. It is sufficient
for God to His satisfaction, joy and glory, as seen in the
burnt-offering which ascended to the Lord as a sweet
smelling savour ; and it is sufficient for man's need to his
salvation and the procuring of every blessing he requires for
time and eternity ; hence, we find every blessing is the product of His blood. Peace is made by His blood, forgiveness
is obtained by His blood, nearness is granted through His
blood, sanctification operates by His blood, victory is possible
by His blood, cleansing comes through His blood, hell is
defeated by His blood, and heaven is certain by the passport
of His blood.

VI. Christ taught that His death would be *complete
in its issue.* He spoke of being " perfected " when referring
to His death and resurrection (Luke xiii. 32), of His death
fulfilling what had been written " concerning " Him (Luke
xxiv. 27, 44), of having " finished " a work which had been
given Him to do (John xvii. 4), of being " straitened " till He
had " accomplished " a " baptism " which He had to pass
through (Luke xii. 50), of that which had been " written by
the prophets " having to be " accomplished " (Luke xviii. 31 ;
xxii. 37), and it was when He was dying on the Cross that
knowing the Scripture must " be fulfilled," and " all things "
. . . " accomplished," that He cried, " It is finished " (John
xix. 24, 28, 30).

" It is accomplished " was Christ's victorious cry on the
cross. There is no suggestion here of a " working force in
us," as some would tell us when they deny His substitutionary
death, but there is undoubtedly something accomplished for
us. Do not the phenomena of the cross suggest some of the
things accomplished ? His prayer for forgiveness for His

enemies announces forgiveness offered to all. His assuring
word to the penitent thief proclaims Paradise is regained.
The three hours' darkness rolled away speaks of the passing
away of the outer darkness for the redeemed, and the light
of a new heaven. The rent veil tells us of the opened way
into the Father's heart. The quaking earth by contrast
heralds forth the things that cannot be shaken. The rent
rocks announce the power of the Cross, the power to rend
the hearts of adamantine sinners from sin. The opened
graves preach the glorious news that the death of Christ has
vanquished death and all its powers. The risen saints and
their appearance to their friends, tell out the reunion of the
sleeping and living saints ; and the confession of the centurion
that Jesus was the Son of God, proclaims the attractive
power of Calvary to win men to the Saviour. Many more
things were accomplished. Law was magnified, justice was
satisfied, hell was stultified, God was glorified, Scripture was
fulfilled, sin's barrier was removed, heaven was opened, and
all blessing was secured. The influence of that glorious work
will vibrate through the universe of God's creation, till all
things shall be harmonised in the will of God. Sin which
caused " a harsh din " to go clanging through the whole of
the fair creation, shall be hushed in Him Who taketh away
the sin of the world.

VII. Christ taught that His death would be *practical in
its outcome*. The objective fact of Christ's vicarious sacrifice
is a subjective force which is vitalising in its working. Listen
to Christ's own words again. He said, " Verily, verily, I say
unto you, except a corn of wheat fall into the ground and
die, it abideth alone, but if it die it bringeth forth much
fruit. He that loveth his life shall lose it, but he that hateth
his life in this world shall keep it unto life eternal. If any
man serve Me, let him follow Me " (John xii. 24-26). The one

dominating thought in these wondrous words is, that as Christ lost His life in blessing us, so we ought to follow Him in being willing to lay down our lives for others ; and as He has found Himself in the ennobled lives He has blest, so we find ourselves in others whom we have served out of love to Him.

Deep in the heart of the Swiss Alps, in the valley of Lauterbrunnen, there is a marvellous cascade known as the Falls of the Staubbach. It is made by little rivulets that come down from a mountain opposite the Jungfrau, from a height of about 5,000 feet. As seen from the Wengern Alp it looks, as it dashes downward, like a string of pearls beading the garments of a monarch. Rounding a thousand curves and angles, it rushes on, when at length, by a sheer leap of nearly a thousand feet, it reaches the valley below. The silver stream becomes less and less defined as it falls, until, about two-thirds of the distance down, it fades into a mere vapour. The torrent seems to fade away, and is lost in mist, and to be lost for ever, hence the name of Staubbach—the " Dust Fall." But these waters, although they vanish, are not lost. They gather themselves together again, for a few rods from the foot of the cliff, where the water seemed to disappear, it reappears again and glides on with a gentler flow. What a parable we have in those seeming lost and found waters. They are like the life that knows experimentally, fellowship with Christ in His death. To be crucified with Christ, and to be made conformable to His death means to be dead to self, to have the flame of the crucified burning in the heart, to have the spell of the love of Christ moving us in service for others, to have the nails go through the hands of unrighteousness, to have the spikes piercing the feet of worldly ways, and to have the hands of the pierced One holding ours in hallowed fellowship, causing us as we feel the dented palms to praise Him with grateful love.

The Gospel according to modern thought teaches, as we have already seen, " The remission of penalty does not depend upon Christ, but is obtained through the incorporation of His own life with the life of the human soul." Contrast that statement with the words of Divine inspiration, where we read, " Christ died for our sins," " Christ bore our sins in His own body on the tree," " He was manifested to take away our sins," " Once in the end of the world He appeared to put away sin by the sacrifice of Himself," and " Christ died for the ungodly." Here is hope for the sinner, salvation for the lost, and an incentive to holiness.

One question which we must all face is, " Shall Christ die in vain ?" It is possible, if we do not avail ourselves of the benefit and blessing of His death. One of the most pathetic letters of the great war was written by a soldier to his sister. This is part of the letter :—

" You know why I'm unhappy. It's not the dying, dear old girl, that worries me, and I know that you are as sure of that, as I am that my number's up. I wouldn't put it so crudely, old lady, if we didn't both feel the truth, and if we couldn't both so honestly, and so humbly, and without hypocrisy say, ' God's will be done.' It was almost a comfort to me when I confessed to you that I know I must face the ' Valley of the Shadow ' in France, and you told me that you had the same premonition. What is it, I wonder, sister mine, this queer, psychic bond of the twin ? Well, anyway, as I said, it's not the dying. I shall be just as jolly, right up to the end, as you will be brave afterwards. Don't tell the mater anything till then. What does worry me as I squat here in my dug-out is whether I shall have died in vain."

Something similar was in the mind of the Apostle when he spoke of Christ dying in vain. He will have died in vain if we do not avail ourselves of His death. He offers Himself in the cleansing of His blood, in the blessing of forgiveness of sins, in the gift of eternal life, in the joy of peace with God, in the separating power of His death, in the victory of His Cross, in the glow of His love, and in the might of His grace. May I put a personal question to any unsaved reader of these lines ? Will you not receive Him now by an act of your will, and thus be saved by Him, and made holy in Him ?

> He died, atonement full to make,
>   For sin's dark crime and shame ;
> He knew the claim of God in law,
>   With these in view He came.
> " The soul that sinneth it shall die,"
>   He gave His soul instead :
> Thus God in Christ His claim has met
>   And raised Him from the dead.
>
> He died to put away our sin,
>   The barrier great and tall,
> That kept the God of Love from us,
>   And did our lives enthrall.
> The hell of sin He far removed,
>   And made the way so clear,
> That now we can come near to God,
>   Without a doubt or fear.
>
> He died that sins might be forgiven,
>   His blood the price must be,
> The Life for Life, the sum was paid,
>   To set the sinner free.
> The freedom gained is great and full,
>   For every sinner born,
> And those who will the Christ receive,
>   Shall never be forlorn.

He died, He shed His precious blood,
  To cleanse from sin's foul blot,
To make us white and pure as He,
  And free from sin's dark spot.
He died, that we the right might have,
  Into the Holy Place,
And fellowship with God enjoy,
  And gaze upon His face.

He died that we might know our part,
  With Christ on Calvary's cross,
That we to sin and self might die,
  And count the world as dross.
He died that we might live to Him
  In holy deed and life,
For Calvary's flame inspires to love
  And ends unholy strife.

He died to bruise the serpent's head,
  And all his works destroy,
That in His triumph we might share,
  And all its fruit enjoy.
He died that we might serve Him well,
  In all we do and say,
And in the world His name confess,
  And ever own His sway.

He died to consecrate entire,
  Our spirit, body, soul,
He died to make us like Himself,
  And all our life control.
He died that He might come again,
  Us to Himself receive,
And share with Him the glory bright,
  Who on His name believe.

2

Comprehensiveness of Christ's Atonement

Dr. Hugh McMillan says: "The Atonement of our Lord is the grandest and most distinctive thing in the Bible— for the sake of which, indeed, the Bible was produced. Very superficial must be the study of the natural and human worlds, that overlooks the vast concurrent testimony which they give to this vital truth. In certain of its aspects, the Atonement is no unique doctrine, no startling theme. The oldest fact of nature, the inmost fact of society, the greatest fact of Christianity meet and are one on Calvary." I have no hesitation in saying, the Atonement is not only "the greatest fact of Christianity,"

IT IS CHRISTIANITY

It is the supplier of all human need, the answerer of all human questions, the minister to all human ills, the joy of all human sorrows, the remover of all human guilt, and the securer of all Divine glory. Dryden has aptly and happily expressed it when he said:

"Look humbly upward, see His will disclose,
The forfeit first, and then the fine impose;
A mulct thy poverty could never pay,
Had not eternal wisdom found the way,
And with celestial wealth supplied thy store;
His justice makes the fine, His mercy quits the score.
See God descending in the human frame,
The offended suffering in the offender's name:
All thy misdeeds to Him imputed see,
And all His Righteousness devolved on thee."

In these studies on this theme of themes in the pages
of Holy Writ, and by the inner illumination of the Holy
Spirit, I trust we shall come to this conclusion—

"CHRIST DID NOT DIE FOR NOTHING, NOR FOR SOMETHING MERELY, BUT FOR EVERYTHING"

I. *Christ in His Atonement is the Sum of All Knowledge.* The essence of Greek philosophy was, "O, man
know thyself." The sum of the gospel is, "This is life
eternal, to know Thee, the only true God; and Jesus Christ,
Whom Thou hast sent." Why was He sent? Christ Himself
answers the question—"I have glorified Thee on the earth,
I have finished the work which Thou gavest Me to do."
Thus the sum of the gospel is, to know Christ in His accomplished work on the cross, and, by knowing Him, to know
God in the provision of His love, and the saving of His
grace. He who knows not the Christ of Calvary knows not
God, and he who does not thus know, knows not anything
that is worth knowing. Adolph Saphir says: "To know
Jesus Christ, and Him crucified, is not the minimum of
knowledge, but the maximum of knowledge . . . it is
not to know little, but to know all; here is not a descent
from a loftier region, but an elevation to the highest sanctuary. In Jesus Christ and Him crucified all doctrines, all
God's teachings, and man's experiences culminate; and
from Jesus Christ and Him crucified all duties, all works,

ALL MINISTRIES ARE TO CULMINATE AND TO BE EVOLVED

Here is the hidden and perfect wisdom of God. No doctrine is seen clearly and truly unless it leads to the cross:
no work is God-pleasing, and no experience or attainment

genuine and vital, unless it has its source, root, and strength in the Cross; no waiting for the Second Advent is healthy and purifying unless it is called forth by the contemplation of the Great God and Saviour, Who gave Himself for us, and redeemed us from all iniquity. O blessed concentration! Blessed simplicity of the gospel! From this centre, from this Cross of Jesus Christ, as from the heart, are the issues of life."

II. *Christ in His Atonement is the Substantiation of all Prophecy.* Take away the theme of Christ's substitutionary work from the Old Testament, and the whole of it falls to the ground. See it there, and then it becomes a living body, through which the Blood of Atonement is pulsating from the heart of God's love all the time. Take one chapter, Isaiah liii., that Quarry where the gold of Christ's Atonement is predicted, proclaimed, and illustrated, and let us ponder seven words, and couple with them seven New Testament words, and, as we do so, we shall find that the Old Testament lies open in the New, as the New Testament is hidden in the Old.

"HE HATH *borne* OUR GRIEFS"

"HE *bare* THE SIN OF MANY" (Isaiah liii. 4, 12).

"WHO HIS OWN SELF *bare* OUR SINS" (I. Peter ii. 24).

The thought in each of these verses is, Christ bearing our sins up to the tree in order to bear them away, as the sacrificial victim was led to the altar as a substitute, to be put to death. Luther strongly put it when he says: "God laid upon Him our sins . . . . saying, 'Be Thou Peter the denier; Paul the persecutor, blasphemer, and cruel oppressor; that sinner that ate the fruit in Paradise; that thief which hanged upon the cross; and, briefly, be Thou the sinner who hath committed the sin of all.' "

"*Carried* OUR SORROWS" (Isaiah liii. 4).

"Lamb of God, Which *taketh away* the Sin of the World" (John i. 29).

The word *"carried"* is the same as *"bear"* in Isaiah liii. 11—*"Bear* their iniquities," and means to bear a heavy burden. It is rendered *"to bear"* in Genesis xlix. 15 in speaking of Issachar, and comparing him to a couching ass —couching as a strong ass between two burdens. What a striking illustration of Christ, with the burden of our sins upon Him, and the burden of God's wrath against them. The word which John uses means to lift up a burden upon oneself, and then to carry it away.

"Wounded for Our Transgressions (Isa. liii. 5).

"Him Whom They *Pierced"* (John xix. 37).

The word *"wounded"* means to bore, to torment (margin), and to slay. It might be rendered "He was pierced for our transgressions." The same word occurs in Psalm cix. 22—"My heart is *wounded* within me." It is interesting to know that the same thought meets us in connection with the meat offering. We read of "unleavened cakes" (Leviticus ii. 4). Newberry renders it *"pierced* cakes," and in the margin of his Bible he has this note— "Hebrew, *Chaloth,* from *Chahlal,* to be pierced or wounded." *Chahlal* is the word rendered *"wounded"* in the above passages. The Arab oven was a large, broad vessel, in the bottom of which sharp flints were set. The cake placed upon these flints became indented, and was thus baked. It is difficult to imagine a type of suffering more forcible than this. The Psalmist, in speaking of the wicked, says, "Thou shalt make them as a fiery oven in the time of Thy wrath" (Psa. xxi. 9). Christ, because of our transgressions, was placed in the oven of God's wrath, and felt the flints of His judgment. He now bears the marks, in His marked hands and feet and side, of that indenting work.

"Bruised FOR OUR INIQUITIES"
"IT PLEASED JEHOVAH TO *bruise* HIM" (Isaiah liii. 5, 10).
"CHRIST HATH ONCE *suffered* FOR SINS"
(1. Peter iii. 18).

The word *"bruise"* does not convey all the intensity of the one used. *"Crushed"* is the more expressive word. The following uses of the word illustrate. The word is translated *"to crush"* in Lamentations iii. 34, as when one is trampled under foot; *"to break in pieces"* in Psalm lxxii. 4, and *"to beat in pieces"* in Isaiah iii. 15, as when an image is completely smashed; and it also signifies to be *"smitten"* (Psalm cxliii. 3), *"broken"* (Psalm lxxxix. 10), and *"to destroy"* (Job vi. 9), as when one is smitten to the ground, then broken, and ground to powder. Christ, to save us from the consequences of our iniquities, was ground in the mills of God's terrible wrath. No wonder it is said He suffered . He was sore *"vexed."* The word *"suffered"* is rendered *"vexed"* in Matt. xvii. 15, and *"felt"* in Acts xxviii. 5. His sufferings were not imaginary nothings, but terrible and awful realities. His were the pains, the bruisings, that ours might be the blessings and the pleasures.
"THE *Chastisement* OF OUR PEACE WAS UPON HIM"
(Isaiah liii. 5).
"MADE PEACE BY THE BLOOD OF HIS CROSS"
(Colossians i. 20).

Here again the word *"chastisement"* does not convey all that is signified. Alexander renders it *"punishment."* The word is often translated *"correction"* in referring to a father punishing his children; hence, the "rod of *correction"* and the *"correction"* of the stocks are essential in their discipline (Prov. vii. 22; xxii. 15). The word is also rendered *"Bond"* in Job xii. 18, *"check"* in Job xx. 3, and *"Rebuker"* in Hosea v. 2. What a bond He was in, what

a check of reproach He received, and what a Rebuker of
sin He found the Righteous God to be when He suffered
on our account. "Punishment!" Peace! What two oppo-
sites. Punishment for Him. Peace for us. Peace means
to bind together, to make one. The word *"peace"* is translated *"one"* in Acts vii. 26. We are made one with God's
blessing because Christ was made one with our punishment.

"By His *stripes* We Are Healed" (Isaiah liii. 5).

"By Whose *stripes* Ye Were Healed" (1. Peter ii. 24).

The word *"stripes"* means to scar, and comes from a
root which means to join, as Newberry says, *"Scar,
Chaburah,* from *Chabar,* to join."* The root word signifies
to have fellowship with, to couple together. It is rendered
"coupled together" in speaking of the curtains of the
Tabernacle (Exodus xxvi. 3). He was joined to our sin
in having joined to Him the punishment that was due to
it; and we who believe in Him are now joined in His benefit, for, in His death for us, we have died with Him. We
receive the wealth of His Atonement, since He has received
the weals of our desert.

"Laid on Him the Iniquity of us all" (Isaiah liii. 6).

"Made Him to be Sin for us" (11. Cor. v. 21).

"He caused to meet upon Him" is Newberry's more
expressive reading. Alexander says, "The Common Version is objectionable only because it is too weak, and suggests the idea of a mild and inoffensive gesture, whereas
that conveyed by the Hebrew word is necessarily a violent
one." The use of the word illustrates its forcible significance. It is used of a bear meeting a man—"a bear *met*
him" (Amos v. 19), of a person assailing another to kill
him—"he *fell* upon him that he died" (1. Kings ii. 25), of
something which separates as when a cloud hides from
view—"the cloud that *cometh betwixt"* (Job xxxvi. 32).

Christ was the One upon Whom the mass of human guilt came as a wild beast to tear Him to His hurt and death, and our iniquity was the great obscurer to cause Heaven's face to be hidden from Him. He was the personification of sin, and we who are His are now represented in all the perfection of His Divine Humanity.

We might dwell upon other words in this wonderful Old Testament quarry, where the gold of Christ's Atonement is to be found, but the above, with their practically corresponding New Testament statements, are sufficient to show how the one is concealed in the other, and the other lies open in the one.

III. *Christ's Atonement is the Basis of all His Offices.* Christ's official positions are generally summed up under Prophet, Priest, and King. As we think of Him in this three-fold office, the Scripture-guided mind naturally turns to the Gospels in thinking of Him as Prophet; to the Epistle to the Hebrews in pondering His Priesthood; and to the Book of Revelation in relation to His future glory as King.

CHRIST, AS THE PROPHET

was ever seeking to impress upon His disciples that He had come into the world to die. Instead of sweeping the starry heavens of Christ's whole teaching, let us concentrate our thought upon the pleiades of His testimony as found in John x. The sum of His teaching is, He had come to give life to His sheep. How was that life to be communicated? By His death: "I lay down My life," is His repeated statement (verses 15, 17, 18). He does it voluntarily, although He is acting under His Father's direction (verse 18), but He does it "*for* the sheep." The emphasis is on the preposition "*for*." The preposition in verses 11 and 15 signifies "*on behalf of*." He makes a provision in His death, which meets the necessity of the sheep; hence, He acts on their behalf as a shepherd does, who loses his life in rescuing one of his flock. Thus we find from the teaching of Christ, His "death is not an incident in His life, it is the aim of it. The laying down of His life is not an accident in His career, it is a vocation; it is that in which the Divine purpose of His life is revealed."

Christ made an earnest effort to instil into the minds of His disciples that He came into the world to die, but they failed to apprehend His teaching (Mark viii. 31; ix. 31; x. 32) until after His resurrection (Luke xxiv. 25, 44). There was only one who seemed to enter into the purpose of His life, and that one was Mary of Bethany. She anointed Him for His burial (John xii. 7); but apart from her, Christ had to go to heaven's inhabitants to talk about His decease which He should accomplish at Jerusalem (Luke ix. 31).

CHRIST, AS THE PRIEST

did not enter upon His office as Priest until after His death. Although His offering of Himself was a priestly act, He did not act as a Priest, but as an Offerer. He offered Himself without spot to God. He had no right to act as a priest on earth, not being of the tribe of Levi and of the house of Aaron (Hebrews vii. 14, viii. 4). It is most important to apprehend the difference between Christ's atonement and priesthood.

Atonement is a thing of death. Priesthood is a ministry of life.

Atonement is finished. Priesthood is continuous.

Atonement was accomplished on earth. Priesthood is carried on in heaven.

Atonement is for the sinner. Priesthood is for the saint.

The main thing to which attention is directed is, Christ did not enter into the Holy Place to exercise His ministry by the blood of animals, but "by His own blood" (Heb. ix. 12). The force and significance of the sentence, "by His own blood," is on the preposition *"dia,"* rendered *"by."* It means, "by means of"; that is, His right of entry into the presence of God, to appear there as our Representative and Priest, is found in His own blood. Saphir remarks: "When He entered into the Holy of Holies, it was by virtue of the blood which He had shed on the cross; it was not by virtue of His love and grace, His priestly spirit and life on earth that He entered into the Heavenly Sanctuary. . . . His whole priestly office is based on His death on the cross."

CHRIST, AS POTENTATE

will reign because of His death. The Book of the Revelation is the Book of coming glory and judgment, and in that book we read more about the slain Lamb than in any other book. The Lamb is mentioned thirty-two times in the New Testament, and out of that number twenty-eight occur in Revelation. The Book opens by describing a Lamb on the throne bearing the marks of death. The Book describes a multitude washed in the blood of the Lamb; it speaks of the Lamb slain from the foundation of the world; it represents a band of overcomers through the blood of the Lamb; and ends by saying the Lamb is the Light of the New Jerusalem. Dr. Denney says of Christ in Revelation: "Here the Lamb is represented as Sovereign—the Object of all praise; as a Lamb which had been sacrificed—the sentence means, 'with the throat cut'; as living and victorious—standing. It has the character which sacrifice

confers, but it is alive; it is not dead, but it has the virtue
of its death in it. It is on the ground of His death, and
of the redemption effected by it, that all praise is ascribed
to the Lamb, and the knowledge and control of all put into
His hands."

What is the one thing these facts proclaim? It is this—
all Christ had to say pointed to the cross, as the sign-post
points to the city. All God has to give emanates from the
cross, as all light and warmth come from the sun. All
Christ is now doing is founded on the cross, as the building rests upon the foundation; and all that Christ will be
as King is secured by the cross of His atoning sacrifice.
His cross secures His crown. His passion is the price of
His glory.

IV. *Christ in His Atonement is the Sum of all Teaching.*
Turn where we will in the Book we find the Spirit of God,
like Moses pointing to the brazen serpent, draws attention
to the sacrifice of our Lord. Let us take a bird's-eye view
of the Gospel of John, where we find a picture gallery,
in which this one fact is represented in many different
ways. He is the Lamb of God, Who bears away the sin
of the world because He bears it. He is the mighty
Hercules, Who takes the load of our iniquity, and annihi-
lates it in the sea of His atonement (i. 29). He is the
Way cast up from earth to heaven, at the cost of His life,
and now the angels of God's blessings descend to us; and
by Him the angels of our prayers and praises ascend to
God (i. 51). He is the Destroyed Temple, razed to the
ground by the hands of wicked men, but out of which
God creates a spiritual and lasting temple that none can
mar nor destroy (ii. 19). Christ is the Uplifted One, of
whom the uplifted serpent of brass in the wilderness was
but a type. He gives life by His death, and lifting up to

those bowed down by sin (iii. 14). He gives His flesh for the life of the world (vi. 51-53). His flesh and blood are not only the removers of guilt, but the satisfiers of the heart. He is the Door by means of Whom ("By Me" means, by means of Me) we enter into the pastures of His provision and peace (x. 9). The good Shepherd gives Himself for us in death, that He may communicate His life to us. He became identified with us in our sin, by His death, in time, that we might be partakers of His life in its eternalness and energy (x. 10, 28). He is the One about Whom the Holy Spirit made Caiaphas speak, when he said: "It is expedient for us, that one man should die for the people" (xi. 50). The necessity of His death for us is found in the lostness of our condition, for if He died not for us, we perish for ever. He is the Corn of Wheat which must fall into the ground of our death, if we are to live in the fruit of His life (xii. 24). He comes to the hour of all hours in the world's history, and into the trouble and sorrow of all trouble and sorrow, when He exclaims: "Now is My soul troubled," &c. (xii. 27). He knew it was the night of His anguish when Judas betrayed Him. It was not only night in the physical universe, but in the moral and spiritual realm too, so He entered into the night, to bring us into the light (xiii. 30). Even when He is in the light of God's presence, praying His wonderful prayer, the shadow of the cross flits across His path; hence, we hear Him saying: "For their sakes I sanctify Myself" (xvii. 19); and then we reach the climax when He is fixed by the nails to the tree, and still the Spirit emphasises and explains that the pierced Christ is the One of Whom He had spoken at the first. The Paschal Lamb which protected Israel in Egypt, and the Pierced One of the Prophetic Psalm are one and the same. He had no other to teach, no other lesson to give. The Christ of Calvary, the passion of the cross, is the sum of all He has said. And we say:

> "No subject so glorious as He;
> No theme so affecting to us."

V. *Christ in His Atonement is the Substance of all Preaching.* The teaching of the Spirit in the Word about Christ's atonement is to be the substance of our preaching to the world. "The whole secret of Christianity is contained in Christ's death," as Dr. Denney says; or perhaps we might say: "The whole secret is in the Christ that died"; for, while we speak of the atonement of Christ, it is more expressive to speak of Christ in His atonement. The worker in the work, and not the work apart from the worker. Dr. Saphir, in calling attention to Paul's words, "I determined to know nothing among you but Jesus Christ, and Him crucified," says: "He preaches Christ crucified; not the crucifixion. We do not preach the death of Christ as a past event, but the Lord Himself, Who, having offered Himself by the eternal Spirit, is now at the right hand of God, to dispense the blessings which He has purchased with His own blood. We do not go to the cross, but to Jesus the Son of God, Who, through death, entered the Heavenly Sanctuary. From Him we receive the gifts of His grace. He Himself bestows the pardon, which His atonement secured. All the blessings of the New Testament in His blood are sent by the Lord Himself, and they are doubly precious to us, because they come from the exalted Jesus, the same Saviour Whose hands and feet were pierced on the cross." This is the sum and substance of all true preaching, and the right standpoint from which to preach.

When we look through the Acts of the Apostles, we find

the attitude of those who preach is, *they point to the Christ
on the throne in resurrection power, Who was on the cross
in substitutionary death.*   Let us take one of the several
words rendered *"preach,"* and trace it through the Acts
and see how this is brought out.   "The word 'preach' occurs
some 112 times in the New Testament—and means to proclaim"; it is the accepted equivalent for six different Greek
verbs.   Three of these are from a common root, which
means to bear a message or bring tidings.   This statement
covers about sixty cases.   As to the other three Greek
words, one is used over fifty times, and means to publish
or proclaim; another six times, and means to say, speak or
talk about.   The other, which means to dispute or reason,
is the only one which suggests a formal discourse or argu-
ment and this is only used twice.

Let us look at one of these words: the one which signifies
to evangelise, to proclaim glad tidings, and always the glad
tidings about Christ.

"They ceased not to *preach* Jesus as the Christ (R. V.,
v. 42).

"Went everywhere *preaching* the Word" (viii. 4).

"Preaching the things concerning the Kingdom (viii. 12).

"Preached the gospel" (viii. 25).

"Preached unto him Jesus (viii. 35).

"Preaching peace by Jesus Christ (x. 36).

"Preaching the Lord Jesus" (xi. 20).

"Declare unto you glad tidings" (xiii. 32).

"Preached the gospel" (xiv. 7).

"Preach unto you" (xiv. 15).

"Preached the gospel" (xiv. 21).

"Preaching the Word of the Lord" (xv. 35).

"Preach the gospel unto them" (xvi. 10).

"Preached Jesus and the resurrection" (xvii. 18).

If these passages are prayerfully studied they will more or less revolve round a Person, an event, and a purpose. *The purpose* is God's design to bless man through Christ, as indicated in the words and context of Acts xiii. 32, for, as the apostle says, the good tidings which he declared had to do with "the promise which was made unto the fathers"; hence, he proclaimed that "through this Man" forgiveness of sins was obtained. *The event* was the death of Christ in its vicariousness; hence, when the evangelist found the eunuch reading of Christ's life being taken away, he "preached unto him Jesus," from the very Scripture he was reading (Acts viii. 35); and the *Person,* Who was the soul, the sum, and the substance of apostolic testimony from first to last was Christ, for they "ceased not to preach Jesus as the Christ" (Acts v. 42, R. V.)

VI. *Christ in His Atonement is the Centre of all the Graces.* The Holy Spirit has summarized the graces as faith, hope, and love. Faith *looks back* to the cross and sees Christ as the Sin-Bearer; love *looks up* to the throne and sings, "He loved me and gave Himself for me"; and hope *looks on* to the glory and sees the slain Lamb is the Light of it. Faith *rests on* the foundation of Christ's finished work; love *is inspired* by the fire of Calvary; and hope *is expectant* of the pierced King. Faith's testimony is, "His atoning blood frees me from sin and rests me about salvation"; love's witness is, "He Who was on the cross is my love"; and hope's jubilant note is, "Through the cross to the light." "Faith goes up the stairs which love has made, and looks out of the window which hope has opened."

There are many passages of Holy Writ which might be taken to illustrate how these three graces centralize and radiate from the cross as the light from the sun, but I

content myself with giving three—(Romans iii. 25; 1. John
iv. 19; and Titus ii. 13, 14).

FAITH'S FOUNDATION

"Whom God hath set forth to be a Propitiation through
faith in His blood" (Romans iii. 25). God's thought of
grace, as well as our act of faith, centralizes and rests in
the atonement of Christ. God sets Him forth as the Propitiation or Mercy Seat. The Mercy Seat was the place
where atonement was made, so we might read for propitiation "the price of expiation." The price is the blood;
expiation is the result, Godward; and redemption is the
result of our faith in the Expiator. We must make much
of Him, when we see the meaning of His death, as one has
said: "Looking upon the Crucified . . . you understand
the joy with which, from age to age, men have spoken
of a death which is their life, of a cross which is their
crown and glory. You are in no mood to disparage the
doctrine of the atoning blood; to place it in the back-
ground of your Christianity; to obscure the cross behind
even the roofs of Bethlehem."

Faith can find no rest but in the cross of Christ's atonement, even as Noah's dove could find no resting-place for
her foot but in the ark, when Noah first sent her out. The
object of faith is Christ in the foundation of His atonement; the *ground of faith* is Christ in the assurance of His
Word; the *growth of faith* is dependent upon Christ as its
Root; the *atmosphere of faith* is the love of Christ; the
character of faith is moulded by Him Who is the Author
and Finisher of faith; the *food of faith* is the Christ in His
promises; and the *expression of faith* is obedience to Him
Who loved even to death.

LOVE'S INSPIRATION

"We love, because He first loved us" (1. John iv. 19, R. V.). How did He love? The Son of God Who loved us, and gave Himself up for us, even we who had given ourselves up to sin. The holding power which enabled Him to give Himself up to such a terrible death for us was His love. That love is the fire that kindled our affection. George Eliot says: "'Tis what I love determines how I love." The believer loves the *"what"* because of the *"who."* The cross is precious because of the Christ. That giving up makes our giving up easy. That sacrifice moves us to sacrifice. That passion kindles a like flame.

> Love is our life,
> The blood that courses through the heart
> And vibrates in all.

HOPE'S CONCENTRATION

"Looking for that blessed hope . . . Who gave Himself for us" (Titus ii. 13, 14). The spring of hope flows from the Smitten Rock. The bright outlook of hope is possible because of the eminence of Calvary's Mount. Longfellow says:

"Thoughts of Him to-day have oft been borne inward
　　upon me,
　Wherefore I do not know, but strong is the feeling
　　within me
That once more I shall see a face I have never forgotten."

We can never forget that face that was marred for us. The gory clots of Gethsemane are the glory spots of our blessing. The wound-prints are prophetic hints of glory tints.
Our faith can never be weak, our love small, nor our

hope dim, as we know the Christ of Calvary, as Saphir says:
"Jesus Christ crucified. See here the foundation of our
faith, the source of our love, the spring of our hope."

VII. *Christ in His Atonement is the Medium of all
Blessing.* There is one expression which is frequently
used in describing the Lord Jesus as the medium by Whom
blessing comes to us, and that is,

"THROUGH OUR LORD JESUS CHRIST,"

or an equivalent term. The preposition *"dia"* means more
than *"through,"* as by a channel, like a pipe being the
medium by which the water in the cistern flows to the tap;
the word denotes, as found in connection with Christ, an
active agent, therefore the expression, *"By means of,"* better conveys the sense. Dr. Bullinger, in his Greek *Lexicon,*
says: *"Dia,* with genitive, through (as proceeding from),
through (by means of), marking the agency, or instrument,
of an action." It is impossible to turn to a tithe of the
Scriptures where blessings are said to come "through our
Lord," or by means of His death. Let us turn to Romans
v. and note seven blessings:

"PEACE"

"Peace with God *through* our Lord Jesus Christ" (ver.
1). Christ is the Peace-maker, and we are, by our faith,
the peace-takers. The Shiloh waters of God's peace flow
from the stricken rock of Calvary, and we come with the
cup of our faith and slake our thirst as we partake of Him.

"ACCESS"

"Through Whom also we have had our access by faith
into this grace wherein we stand" (Romans v. 2, R. V.)
Christ went into the distance and darkness of our deserving

and we are brought into the faultlessness of His perfection
and the fulness of His grace by means of His procuring
death.

SALVATION

"We shall be saved from wrath *through* Him" (verse 9).
The wrath is prospective, looming in the distance like an
approaching storm about to break upon the sinner to his
confusion and condemnation, but by means of Him Who
has been condemned for us, we stand where no judgment
can ever reach us.

RECONCILIATION

"Reconciled to God *through* the death of His Son" (verse
10, R. V.). To be reconciled means to have one's feelings
changed towards another. Christ did not come to reconcile
God to us, but God was in Christ reconciling *us* to Himself.
This change has been wrought by God in Christ. His love
has conquered our enmity.

JOY

"We also rejoice in God *through* our Lord Jesus Christ,
through Whom we have now received the reconciliation"
(verse 11, R. V.). Spurgeon says: "There is a sweet joy
which comes to us through sorrow;" especially is that true
in the joy which is born of Calvary's sorrow. Our Easter
is blithe with joy, because Calvary's night was black with
sorrow.

"LIFE"

"Reign in life *through* the One, even Jesus Christ" (ver.
17, R.V.). As natural life is the union of spirit and body,
so spiritual life is the union of the Lord and the believer.
Life is consciousness of being, so the believer can say, "I
know Him Whom I have believed." This life of union

comes through Christ's death. The corn of wheat having fallen into the ground and died, is no longer alone. The life to which reference is made is comprehensive; it not only refers to present blessing, but future glory.

" RIGHTEOUSNESS "

Dr. Moule renders verse 18: "*Through* one deed of righteousness." What deed? He comments: "It seems . . . possible to explain the word here of the Lord's atoning act, satisfying the law for us, and of the accepting 'act and deed' of the Father, declaring Him accepted, and us in Him."

It will be seen that every one of these blessings centralises in the death of Christ, like the spokes of a wheel in the hub. All blessings, like the sun's beneficent rays, emanate from the sun of Christ's atoning death. Dr. Saphir aptly remarks: "Christ crucified by our sins brings to us God in the fulness of love; brings us to God in the fulness of righteousness. As our life begins at the cross, so, throughout our new life, Christ crucified is the centre of our love and faith."

"The only thing I want," said Bishop Hamilton in his dying moments, "is to place my whole confidence more and more perfectly in the precious blood." We may well say, "The blood of Christ is the only thing we want, for everything is in Him Who shed it." As illustrating how Christ in His atonement is everything and does everything, ponder the following Bible Reading. It *averts* the judgment of God against sin, as the blood of the paschal lamb did on the night of the Passover (Exodus xii. 13; 1. Cor. v. 7). It *converts* the one who believes in the Substitute, even as the blood of cleansing changed the position and condition of the cleansed leper (Leviticus xiv. 14). It *inverts* the position we once occupied in relation to the world, for instead of being in it, we are now separated from it, even as God said to Pharaoh of Israel: "I will put a redemption (margin) between thy people and My people (Ex. viii. 23). The blood *inserts* us into a new place, even as the blood of the covenant enabled Moses and the elders to draw nigh and see the God of Israel (Ex. xxiv. 5-10). The blood *asserts* that the blessings of pardon (Ephesians i. 7), peace (Colossians i. 20), power (Rev. xii. 11), purity (1 John i. 7), and paradise are secured in Him (Rev. vii. 14). The blood *exerts* a powerful influence in its practical bearing, for it kills sin (Rom. vi, 1-15), slays self (11. Corinthians v. 15), and overcomes pride (Phil. ii. 5-8); and the blood of Christ *subverts* the powers of hell, which have been conquered by His death, even as the Philistines were defeated when the sacrificial lamb was offered up (1 Sam. vii. 9, 10; Hebrews ii. 14; Colossians ii. 15).

We might say a good deal more in a general way, but this introductory lecture will suffice to show the importance and place of the atonement of Christ. If we are right about His finished work, we shall be right everywhere. If we are wrong here, we are wrong everywhere.

3

The Meaning of Christ's Atonement

The Atonement as such, is only mentioned once in the New Testament. "We have now received the Atonement" (Romans v. 11), and here the word should be *reconciliation*, and is so rendered in 11. Corinthians v. 18, 19. The word "Atonement" is an Old Testament word, therefore it is to the Old Testament we turn to find its meaning; for while we have the truth of the Gospel in the New Testament, its roots are found in the Old Testament.

Every Bible student recognizes the importance of understanding the words of the Holy Spirit, for if we would know the mind of the Spirit, we must understand the words of the Spirit. "Words . . . which the Holy Ghost teacheth" (1. Corinthians ii. 13) is what the Lord says. Words are the medium by which He communicates His thoughts, hence, the importance of rightly apprehending the words He uses in His Word. We read of the seven lamps in the Tabernacle, that they gave "light over against the candlestick" (Numbers viii. 2). The lamps not only lighted up the Holy Place, but revealed the beauty of the lampstand too. So the light of the truth reveals the truth of the light. The Spirit and the Word are inseparable.

When men apart from the Word try to understand the Word "Atonement," they divide it into its syllables and spell it at-one-ment, which signifies reconciliation, that is, to make two parties at variance, one. This is a result of the Atonement, and not the Atonement itself. Tyndal makes this mistake when he says, "Atonement—to set at one."

A safe rule to follow is to find out the first time a word

is used, and invariably the context will explain its meaning. The Hebrew word *"Caphar,"* a primary root, first occurs in Genesis vi. 14, in speaking of the ark, when God said to Noah, *"Pitch* it within and without with *pitch."* Literally, it is "Thou shalt *caphar* it within and without with a *copher."* Thus both the verb and the noun are used. We might freely render the sentence, "Thou shalt *atone* the ark within and without with an *atonement."* At once the meaning is obvious, namely, "Cover the ark with a *covering."* Thus the word Atonement means to cover. Dr. A. A. Hodge, in his "Outlines of Theology," has finely put it, he says, "The Hebrew word *caphar*—to cover by an *expiatory sacrifice.* . . . Its proper meaning is to make moral and legal reparation for a fault or injury. In its Old Testament and proper theological usage, it expresses not the reconciliation effected by Christ, but the legal satisfaction which is the ground of that reconciliation."

Atonement, therefore, *expresses what Christ gave to God on our behalf,* and hence, He does not see us, as the Irish boy said—"God cannot see my sins through the blood of Christ."

Canon Girdlestone calls attention to the fact that the preposition which is used in connection with atonement expresses a covering. He says, "The Hebrew prepositions rendered by the word 'for' in connection with the doctrine of acceptance and atonement do not mean *instead of,* but *because of,* or *on account of.* The preposition which means *substitution* is never used in connection with the word *caphar.* To make an atonement for a sin is literally to cover *over* the sin, the preposition being constantly used with verbs signifying to cover, *e.g.,* in Hab. ii. 14—"As the waters cover the sea."

Let us call to mind a few Scriptures by way of illustration, where the word to cover occurs: The Flood covering the mountains—"All the high hills were *covered*" (Genesis vii. 19). The mountains were *covered*" (Genesis vii. 20). The flood of Christ's atoning death covers the mountains of our guilt. Where sin abounded, grace did much more abound. Not a mountain of our sin can be seen. The far-reachingness of His atonement covers all.

The Red Sea covering the Egyptians—"The waters *covered* all the host" (Ex. xiv. 28). "The depths have *covered* them" (Exodus xv. 5). The sin which once gripped us and pursued us, is annihilated as an active antagonising force in the Red Sea of His death. Sin is a dead thing to those who know they are crucified with Christ.

The Seraphs covering themselves—"Six wings, with twain he *covered* his face, and with twain he *covered* his feet" (Isaiah vi. 2). The covering wings of His expiation covers all the activities of our service. The covered face of our love can see better, and the covered feet of our service run swifter, because we are in Christ.

The cloud of incense covering the mercy seat—"Cloud of the incense may *cover*" (Lev. xvi. 13). The sweet perfume of Christ's atonement makes the golden perfection of all that relates to Jehovah the more beautiful and bright.

Rebekah covering herself with her vail—"Therefore she took a vail and *covered* herself" (Genesis xxiv. 65). The beauty of Rebekah's graces needs to be hidden in the presence of the Divine Isaac. We can look at Him better when covered with the vail of His humiliating death.

God's grace regarding Israel—"*Covered* thy nakedness. . . . *Covered* thee with silk" (Ezekiel xvi. 8, 10). The covering with which He hides our sin and shame is no common one, it is "silk." Beautiful, costly, soft, and pure. The best robe which covers us was woven in the loom of

Calvary and purchased with Heaven's blood. His atonement is our adornment.

God's glory in the heavens—"His glory *covered* the heavens" (Hab. iii. 3). The garnishing of our heaven is glorious with the sun which was obliterated at the cross, with the Star of Bethlehem, and the blue of God's grace.

Remembering the association of this word, has it not a new meaning when we read such passages as these?

"Blessed is the man whose sin is *covered*" (Psalm xxxii. 1).

"Thou hast *covered* all their sin" (Psalm lxxxv. 2).

"Love *covereth* all sin" (Prov. x. 12).

Let us now return to the word *"atonement,"* and ponder some of its usages. The verb is rendered *"appease," "pitch," "pacified," "purged," "disannulled," "put off,"* and *"make an atonement."*

"PITCH"

In order that the waters of judgment might be kept out of the ark, and those who were inside might be protected, it was covered within and without with pitch. "Pitch it within," &c. (Genesis vi. 14).

Newberry renders, "Pitch, to cover, to make atonement." Rotherham's translation is, "Cover within and without with pitch." As there was a double covering for those in the ark, a covering of atonement without and a covering within, so Christ covers us without from the judgment due to our sin by His death, and covers our sin within. Thus Christ's Atonement covers what we are, and keeps from us what we deserve, for as the judgment of water fell upon the pitch, so Christ endured what was due to us. Spurgeon says, "Christ's merit covers our demerit." "Cover" is the Old Testament word for expiation and propitiation, and we rejoice in it, notwithstanding the opposition of philosophy, falsely so called. Yet let no man wickedly say that 'imputed righteousness is a clean glove which covers a foul hand,' for whom the Lord covers He cleanses."

"APPEASE"
(Genesis xxxii. 20)

When Jacob was about to meet his brother Esau, the consciousness of how he had robbed him of his blessing and birthright filled Jacob with dread. He, therefore, determined to appease his brother's probable anger with a present. The present was a costly one, and consisted of "two hundred she goats, and twenty he goats, two hundred ewes, and twenty rams, thirty milch camels, with their colts, forty kine, ten bulls, twenty she asses and ten foals." We are not left in any doubt as to the intent of the present, for we read, "I will appease him* with the present that goeth before me, and afterward I will see his face; peradventure he will accept of me. So went the present over before him." Rotherham renders the passage, "I must pacify him with the present that goeth on before me, and after that I will see his face." In a footnote on the word "pacify" he remarks, "Lit., 'cover over his face.'" The thought in Jacob's heart was, I will put the present between my brother and myself, that it may cover my offence, that his attention may be diverted from myself to the gift-offering, thus his anger may be pacified. Christ's Atonement is that which has gone before us, which has given satisfaction for us, and now we are completely covered by it, so God does not see our past sins, nor the sinner who committed them.

"PACIFIED"
(Ezekiel xvi. 63)

Jehovah in promising to bless those to whom Ezekiel is

---

*Dean Payne Smith says, "I will cover his face with the offering that goeth before me. The covering of the face of the offended person, so that he could no longer see the offense, became the usual legal word for atonement," speaking, says, it shall be "when I am *pacified* toward thee for all that thou hast done." Newberry renders, "Pacified on the ground of atonement." Rotherham translates, "I have accepted a propitiary-covering for thee as to all that thou hast done." Many object to the thought that Christ gave to God His life to pacify Him, because it suggests the heathenish conception that He had to give Him something in order to bless us. But such a thought is foreign to the passage before us, for God Himself is the Provider of the Atonement which gives Him satisfaction. We must never forget that God is a righteous Ruler as well as a Holy Father, and while He has a heart of love, He has also a hand of righteousness. He placates His righteousness in the death of His Son, in smiting our sin and us in Christ's death, that He might provide for our salvation. The satisfaction Christ and God have given to justice is the satisfaction that satisfies our hearts. Hodge says, "The Atonement was the effect, not the cause of God's love. It satisfied His justice, and rendered the exercise of His love consistent with His righteousness." God in Christ met a requirement of His own throne, that He might provide a redemption consistent with His own nature.

Therefore we rest "upon His justice" for our salvation, as the Scotch body replied, when she was asked what she was resting in for her soul's salvation.

"PURGED"
(Isaiah vi. 7)

"Thy sin is *purged*," was the assuring word of the Seraph to the prophet. "Atoned for," or "covered," as Newberry renders it. Rotherham renders it, "This hath touched thy lips, thus shall be taken away thine iniquity, and thy sin by propitiation be covered." Mark the *"this"* and the *"thus."* The *"this"* has reference to the live coal from off the altar. What does that live coal signify? Fire which had fed upon the sacrifice, which sacrifice had been accepted by God. The *"thus"* speaks of the application of the accepted sacrifice to the man who had confessed his sin, which took away his actual sin, and the propitiation covered the sinner. Therefore the sinner is not seen, but the atonement; and the iniquity does not exist, for it is "taken away," or departed. The word *"taken away"* is translated *"depart"* in Exodus viii. 11, 29, in speaking of the removal of the frogs and flies which plagued Egypt.

"DISANNULLED"
(Isaiah xxviii. 18)

"Your covenant with death shall be *disannulled,"* or *"wiped out,"* as Rotherham gives it. The reference is to the ancient method of writing covenants. They were engraven on stones, and if a covenant was to be annulled, the stone was smeared with a substance which completely obliterated the words from view. Sin has cut itself into our nature, and written itself large upon our being, the consequence is we are covenanted with death, but the power which disannuls is the death of our Lord, which wipes out all the dread and damning consequence of sin. The woundprints of the Christ of Calvary cover the sin-prints of the engraving of hell.

Old Candace in Mrs. Stowe's book aptly puts it when she is represented as comforting another. She says: "Jest leave him in Jesus' hands. Why, honey, dar's de very print o' de nails in His hands now! Look right at Jesus. Don't ask no questions, and don't go to no reasonin's. Jest look at Him hangin' dar, so sweet and patient on de cross. All dey could do couldn't stop His lovin' 'em. He prayed for 'em with all de breath He had. Dar's a God to love, a'n't dar? Candace loves Him, poor, ole, foolish, black, wicked Candace, and she knows He loves her."

"PUT OFF"
(Isaiah xlvii. 11)

"Mischief shall fall upon thee: thou shalt be unable to *put* it *off*" (R. V., *"Expiate,"* Rotherham, *"appease"*). Here the Lord declares the Chaldeans will be unable to appease the mischief which shall come upon them. No help they may summon, nor enchantment they may perform, will shelter them from the punishment which will surely overtake them. What an illustration this is of the sinner's inability to avert the punishment he deserves by any action of his own. Toplady felt this when he sang—

> "Could my zeal no respite know,
> Could my tears for ever flow,
> All for sin could not atone;
> Thou must save, and Thou alone."

Elihu proclaimed this fact to Job long ago. He said to him, "I have found a *Ransom*" (Job xxxiii. 24). Newberry renders Ransom, *"Atonement"*; and he is right in so doing, for it is the Hebrew word *"copher."* "Copher" is rendered *"villages"* in 1. Samuel vi. 18. What is a village? a place where people live. Homes. Shelter. God Himself has provided a village, a shelter, a home in the atonement of Christ. We cannot put off the punishment our sin deserves; but since our Surety has smarted for us, God cannot put any punishment on us.

"MAKE AN ATONEMENT"

This is how the verb *"caphar"* is translated again and again in Leviticus xvi. The word occurs sixteen times. Once it is rendered *"reconciling"* (verse 20). Here again let me take the noun (*"copher"*) to illustrate the verb *"caphar."* Twice the word is translated *"satisfaction"* (Numbers xxxv. 31, 32), and twice *"camphire"* (Song of Solomon i. 14; iv. 13). There were certain offences under the law for which an atonement could not be given, such as murder. But here there is the same thought underlying, that atonement is, as Canon Girdlestone says, "the doing away with a charge against a person by means of expiation, propitiation, or otherwise, so that the accused may be received into the Divine favour, and be freed from the consequence of wrong-doing. Pacification, propitiation, and such words are by no means adequate for the purpose of conveying the doctrine of atonement. They savour too much of heathenism and superstition, and lead to the supposition that man pacifies God instead of teaching that God shelters man; but whatever word is used, the more carefully Scripture is studied, so much the more will the unity, the beauty and the grandeur of God's way of mercy commend itself to the soul."

Mark the words, *"God shelters man,"* for that is the significance of the word *"camphire"* in the Song of Solomon. It may not appear so at first sight, but as the Revised Version says, the reading is, "My beloved is unto me as a cluster of henna flowers in the vineyards of Engedi" (i. 14). The women in the East had a habit of dyeing their lips, hands and cheeks, making them of a saffron, reddish hue. In the British Museum to-day may be seen a mummy's hand so dyed, and with the intimation that it is so coloured by the juice from the henna flower. The women, by applying this stain, got a colouring which made them appear what they were not. The thought is still present, as in every other instance, that *"copher"* and *"capher"* mean to cover. Mr. Spurgeon once said, "Christ is our

Atonement and Adornment." May I alter by saying, "Christ's Atonement *is* our Adornment."

The essential thing to emphasise is, *there is only one atonement for sin, and that is by means of death.* The one clear word which confirms this is, "For the life of the flesh is in the blood: and I have given it to you upon the altar to make an atonement for your souls: for it is the blood that maketh an atonement for the soul" (Leviticus xvii. 11).

Israel was prohibited from eating anything that had the blood in it, on two grounds—(1) Because the life was in it; (2) because it was the symbol of life substituted for the life of the guilty in atoning sacrifice.

Canon Girdlestone asks the important question, "How was atonement wrought? A spotless victim had to be brought before the Lord to take the place of sinful man. Its death, after the sins of the offerer had been laid upon its head, represented the fact that the innocent must suffer for the guilty. Then came the solemn mystery. The priest, God's agent, must take the blood of the victim and scatter it over God's altar. This process set forth the truth that God and death must be brought into contact through means of Him whom priest and altar typified. The symbol was composite, or many-sided, and its various aspects can only be realised and put together when they are regarded in the light of Christ's death upon the cross. It was not His life that made atonement, but His death."

This lecture would not be complete if we did not consider a relative word, because it has a correspondent in the New Testament. I refer to the word—"mercy-seat." The Hebrew word *"Capporeth"* is derived from *"Caphar,"* and is rendered *"Mercy Seat"* (Exodus xxxv. 12; xxxix. 35), or *"Propitiation."* Dr. Bullinger says, "The mercy seat is so called because of the expiation made once a year on the great day of atonement."

The mercy seat was the lid of the ark, and is a remarkable and suggestive type of Christ as the Propitiatory. It is mentioned twenty-seven times. Briefly let us note its description, and, in a sentence, denote its typical import.

Golden Mercy Seat. "Make a mercy seat of pure gold" (Exodus xxv. 17; xxxvii. 6). Gold is typical of what is Divine. Christ is the God-natured, God-provided, God-fitted mercy seat.

Cherubic Mercy Seat. "Make cherubim of gold . . . in the two ends of the mercy seat" (Exodus xxv. 18; xxxvii. 7). Cherubim represent the administrators of God's righteousness. Christ meets God's righteousness in dying for our sin, and the redemption, which is ours in consequence, is justly given.

United Mercy Seat. "Make cherub . . . of one piece with the mercy seat" (Exodus xxv. 19, R.V.; xxxvii. 8). Christ is the expression of God's Holy Love, His righteous mercy, and His pure grace. God's attributes harmonise in the Christ of Calvary.

Sheltered Mercy Seat. "Cherubim shall spread out their wings on high, covering the mercy seat" (Ex. xxv. 20, R.V; xxxvii. 9). After Christ had gone beneath the waters of Jordan as a sinner, in type answering for sin, the Spirit, in Dove form, lighted upon Him; so Christ's atoning sacrifice is guarded by God's righteousness.

Contemplated Mercy Seat. "Their faces shall look one to another; toward the mercy seat shall the faces of the cherubim be" (Exodus xxv. 20; xxxvii. 9). The high intelligences of heaven not only find an object in Christ's sacrifice which commands their satisfaction, but one which demands their united contemplation.

Law Meeting Mercy Seat. "Thou shalt put the mercy seat above upon the ark; and in the ark thou shalt put the testimony that I shall give thee" (Exodus xxv. 21; xl. 20). The mercy seat hid the law, and is typical of Christ, Who covers the law's claim and the law's sentence for us, for He kept the law in every jot and tittle, and redeems from its curse by dying the death it demanded from the sinner.

Communing Mercy Seat. "There will I meet with thee and will commune with thee from above the mercy seat" (Exodus xxv. 22; xxx. 6). God meets with us in Christ, and we have fellowship with the Father in Him. The cleansing blood and the living Christ maintain us in this fellowship.

Holy Mercy Seat. "Thou shalt put the mercy seat . . . in the most holy place" (Exodus xxvi. 34). Holiness is the habitation of His throne. Christ is the living expression of the holy God. He not only dwells in the holy place, but is the Holy One, Who makes the place holy. Very significantly is it said in 1. Chronicles xxviii. 11, that the holy place is "the place of the mercy seat."

God-manifesting Mercy Seat. "I will appear in the cloud upon the mercy seat" (Lev. xvi. 2). The only place where God is seen is in Christ. He is His express image. He is the living expression of the Divine, and Divine in all His expression.

Cloud-covered Mercy Seat. "Cloud of the incense may cover the mercy seat" (Lev. xvi. 13). The cloud would obscure the Shekinah glory. Deity in its Divine purity cannot be seen; but Deity in Divine humanity is "seen, heard and handled," as John declared.

Blood-sprinkled Mercy Seat. "Sprinkle the blood on the mercy seat, and before the mercy seat . . . seven times" (Leviticus xvi. 14, 15). The blood sprinkled once on the mercy seat is typical of Christ giving Himself for us once for all, and the blood sprinkled seven times before the mercy seat typifies the fact that by means of His death He brings us into a perfect standing before God. He has met God's claim, and He meets our need.

When we turn to the pages of the New Testament, there are eight passages where propitiation is stated or indicated. The corresponding Greek word to the Hebrew one is *"hilasterion,"* and is rendered *"propitiation"* in Romans iii. 25, and *"mercy seat"* in Hebrews ix. 5; it means an expiatory—a place or thing—an atoning victim. As one has said, "The mercy seat is so called because of the expiation made once a year on the great day of Atonement." *"Hilasmos"* is rendered *"propitiation"* in I. John ii. 2; iv. 10; and signifies an expiator. *"Hilaskomai"* means to conciliate, to be propitious. It is rendered *"Be merciful"* in Luke xviii. 13, and *"make reconciliation"* in Hebrews ii. 17. *"Hileos"* means propitious, be merciful, as averting some calamity. It is rendered *"be it far"* in Matthew xvi. 22, and *"merciful"* in Hebrews viii. 12. Let us look at these passages in detail.

God and Propitiation. "Whom God set forth (R.V.M., "Purposed"; margin, "Foreordained") to be a *Propitiation.*" Professor Godet gives a concise comment on the whole topic. He says, "The word 'Propitiatory' belongs to that host of Greek adjectives whose termination signifies *what serves to.* The meaning, therefore, is: What serves to render propitious favourable." That which serves to make God act in righteous mercy toward us, is because He has in His merciful righteousness acted for us in Christ. He foreordained to act in mercy for us, that He might in righteousness bless us. Conybeare and Howson render the passage, "For Him hath God set forth, in His blood, to be a propitiatory sacrifice by means of faith, thereby to manifest the righteousness of God."

Scripture and Propitiation. "The cherubim overshadowing the *mercy seat*" (Heb. ix. 5). *The Speaker's Commentary* suggests that the better word, instead of mercy seat, would be a "propitiatory, or atonement," and, in speaking of the mercy seat in the tabernacle and its associations, adds, "It was the central point of the Divine Presence and manifestations between God and the representative of the people. So in Christ, is the full manifestation of God to man made, and in Him rests . . . the true Shekinah. . . . Among all instruments and symbols of atonement this alone was called the propitiatory as being the most eminent. As on it was made a general atonement for the children of Israel once a year; so Christ Jehovah takes away our sins." The one scarlet thread that runs through the Old and New Testaments, and binds both of them together is the blood of atonement. From one end to the other rings out the truth, all approach to God, and all blessing from Him, is on the ground of sacrifice.

Sins and Propitiation. "He is the *propitiation* for our sins: and not for ours only, but also for the whole world" (1. John ii. 2). Sins are here found in connection with two parties—"the sinner and the saint." God has made no provision for His people to sin, but if they do sin provision has been made. The same propitiatory sacrifice is needed for them as for the unsaved. There is only one ground upon which sins can be forgiven, and only One Person Who is the ground, and He and it are the atonement of Christ. The sins of a believer are more sinful than the sins of a sinner, and Christ in His atonement is the Only One Who can answer for both.

Love and Propitiation. "Herein is love, not that we loved God, but that He loved us, and sent His Son to be the *propitiation* for our sins" (1. John iv. 10). Sin deserves wrath. The wrath of God must feed upon us, or upon One instead of us. Love's provision is faith's protection. God, in His love, gave Christ to be our propitiation, and now He sees not us nor our sins, but Him. He, in the worth of His sacrifice, makes us feel He is worth any sacrifice.

Christ and Propitiation. "A merciful and faithful high priest . . . to make *reconciliation*" (R.V., *"propitiation"*) "for the sins of the people" (Hebrews ii. 17). The Speaker's Commentary says, "Only by atoning for sin could He restore man to his proper relation to God." The Old Testament opens with a flaming sword, brought by man's sin to keep him out of Paradise; and the last mention of a sword in the Old Testament is when it awakes against God's Fellow, and is sheathed in His heart, to atone for sin, that man may be restored to a better Paradise (Genesis iii. 24; Zechariah xiii. 7). Every believer can say—

"Now sleeps that sword for me."

Christ has made reconciliation because He has been made sin. The hand of Christ's death has grasped the excalibur of God's sword, and sunk it for ever beneath the waters of oblivion, as far as the believer is concerned.

Sinner and Propitiation. "God be *merciful* to me a sinner" (Luke xviii. 13). The margin of the Revised Version rightly renders —*"Be propitiated."* Rotherham gives it, "O God! be propitiated unto me, the sinner." He seems to say, "See the blood on the Propitiatory and be propitiated towards me, because of Him Who has made propitiation for me." The mercy of God is God given, blood bought, faith taken and love enjoyed. The mercy of God is from the God of mercy, and is justly given, since Christ has righteously died in our stead.

Israel and Propitiation. "I will be *merciful* to their unrighteousness" (Heb. viii. 12); or, as Rotherham, "Because *propitious* will I be as to their unrighteousness." There is no mercy for any one apart from the Christ of Calvary. When the eyes of Israel are opened they will look upon the pierced One. God's propitiousness flows from the propitiatory of Christ's sacrifice.

Man and Propitiation. When Christ told Peter He must die, Peter, in his mistaken concern, said, *"Be it far* from Thee Lord"; or, as the M.R.V., "God have *mercy* on Thee"; or, as Bullinger, "God be *propitious,* or favourable to Thee." Peter wanted Christ to be kept back from such a calamity as the cross, but that would have been the calamity of all calamities for us, for if He had not died we should have died forever. The calamity of condemnation is far from us, because it was not far from—it came upon—Him.

From all this it will be apprehended what Christ is *to* God for us, and what He is *from* God to us.

What Christ is to God for us. He has answered, and does answer, in every way for our sins; as Newton says, "Atonement, or appeasement, is a work of the Lord Jesus *directed towards God,* whereby by one oblation finished on the cross, He has satisfied forever (*in perpetuity*) the claims of Divine government, and procured for all His believing people, not only pardon, but acceptance, and *rewardableness* according to the value of His own meritorious obedience, which has been presented to God, and accepted by God for them."

What Christ is from God to us. Romans iii. 25, 26, is one of the most comprehensive passages of the gospel. The verses have been called "the marrow of theology"; another has said of them, they are "the brief summary of Divine Wisdom"; and Calvin declares, "That there is not probably in the whole Bible a passage which sets forth more profoundly the righteousness of God in Christ." Godet translates the passage, "Whom He hath established beforehand as the means of propitiation through faith in His blood, for the demonstration of His righteousness on account of the tolerance shown toward sins that were past, during the forbearance of God, for the demonstration of His righteousness at the present time, that He might be just, and the justifier of him who is of the faith of Jesus."

When Cowper's eyes lighted on this passage, while under deep conviction of sin, and in the throes of despair, it brought him comfort, and was the means of his salvation. He had contemplated suicide, and was profoundly agitated, walking up and down in his room. At last he seated himself near the window, and took up a Bible. He says, "The passage which met my eye was the 25th verse of the 3rd of Romans. On reading it I immediately received power to believe. The rays of the Sun of Righteousness fell on me in all their fulness; I saw the complete sufficiency of the expiation which Christ had wrought for my pardon, and entire justification. In an instant I believed, and received the peace of the gospel."

"If," he adds, "the arm of the Almighty had not supported me, I believe I should have been overwhelmed with gratitude and joy; my eyes filled with tears; transports choked my utterance. I could only look to heaven in silent fear, overflowing with love and wonder."

4

The Scriptures and
Christ's Atonement

Francis Turretin speaks of the atonement as the chief part of our salvation, the anchor of faith, the refuge of hope, the rule of charity, the true foundation of the Christian religion, and the richest treasure of the Christian Church. He further remarks, "So long as this doctrine is maintained in its integrity, Christianity itself and the peace and blessedness of all who believe in Christ are beyond the reach of danger; but if it is rejected, or any way impaired, the whole structure of the Christian faith must sink into decay and ruin." He practically says the atonement of Christ is the Christian faith, and so it is.

Remove the atonement from the Bible and we have a casket without the treasure, a body without the spirit, a tree without a root, a house without the foundation, a sky without the sun, a cheque-book without the balance at the bank, and a gospel without the message. Dr. R. Wardlaw has said, "To the mind that can contrive to its own satisfaction to strip the Bible of the doctrine of the atonement by vicarious suffering, it might, in my apprehension, be safely pronounced impossible to convey a Divine discovery at all; there being no terms conceivable which might not, by such a mind, be explained away. Salvation is the lesson of the Bible; and it is salvation by atonement, or substitutionary suffering."

When Christ appeared to the two disciples on the way to Emmaus, and to the eleven in the upper room, He showed to them from the Books of Moses, the Psalms, and the Prophets, that His death was essential. On the heights and in the adjacent vicinity of Nyack-on-Hudson there are a number of springs which may be continually tapped. The springs are there, but they need to be tapped before their refreshingness can be enjoyed. The same is true of the Bible—the springs of the truth of the Word are there, but they have to be found to be known.

Christ has indicated where we may find some of the springs of the atonement, as He intimated to the disciples, when He appeared to them in the upper room, and expounded to them all the things concerning His death, which were written in Moses, the Psalms, and the Prophets. I purpose to turn to one of these books, in each of the sections mentioned.

I. *The Book of Genesis*

We shall turn to the Book of Genesis for illustrations on the first section. Genesis has been called the seed-plot of the Bible, and it is so, for every truth in the Bible is found therein, either directly or indirectly. The truth of Christ's atoning work is typified and illustrated again and again.

THE SLEEPING MAN AND THE BUILDED WOMAN

While Adam slept his side was opened, and from what was taken out of him God builded the woman. When Adam saw Eve he said, "This is now bone of my bone, and flesh of my flesh; she shall be called Ishah (margin), because she was taken out of Ish" (margin, Genesis ii. 21-24). Christ slept a deeper and a more significant sleep than Adam —the sleep of His atoning death. From His riven side the atoning blood flowed, by means of which the Church, His ransomed body, will be formed and united in a closer bond than ever existed between our first parents. It is to this mystic oneness the Holy Spirit refers in Ephesians v. 21-23, when He calls attention to the union that existed between Adam and Eve as typical of it. The sleeping man and the riven side were the essential means for the production of the builded woman and the presented bride. The sleeping man was necessary that the woman should be made, and the living woman was necessary for his completement and helpmeet. She would never have been had it not been for him, and he would not have been satisfied had it not been for her (Gen. ii, 18, 23; 1 Cor. xi, 11, 12). So with Christ and the Church. His sleep of death and riven side of atonement make the redeemed all they are in Him, and yet we are His fulness and completion, which make Him complete. We are not complete without Him, and He is not complete without us, any more than the body is perfect without the head, or the head complete without the body. These spiritual facts are brought out in the Epistles to the Colossians and Ephesians. In the former we are said to be "complete in Him" (Colossians ii. 10), and in the latter the Church is the "fulness of Him, that filleth all in all" (Eph. i. 23).

THE SLAIN ANIMAL AND THE CLOTHED SINNERS

Before Adam and Eve left the garden of Eden, God clothed them in coats of skin (Gen. iii. 21). Their shame was hidden at the expense of another's life. The spoils of death saved them from being the spoils of an eternal death. The words *"skins," "coat,"* and *"clothed"* are full of typical meaning. The word *"skins"* comes from a root which means to flay, to make naked. Christ was stripped that we might be clothed. He was put to shame that we might never be put to shame (Hebrews xii, 2; 1. Peter 2, 24). *"Coats"* is from a root word which means to hide, to cover; and *"clothed"* means to wrap around. Christ hides those who cry, "Let me hide myself in Thee," with the perfection of Himself in His perfect work of atonement. He Who was wrapped in glory in the past eternity, became unwrapped in time of His beauty and dignity, that He might wrap up in His righteousness, acceptableness, and worth.

THE OFFERING BROUGHT AND THE SIN-OFFERING REJECTED (Genesis iv. 3-7)

Cain evidently came in his own way to God (Jude 11). The earth had been cursed because of man's sin (Genesis iii. 17). Cain brought of earth's fruit to Jehovah, and by so doing brought a cursed offering. Abel came in God's way, and therefore met with His approbation (Heb. xi. 4). He confessed, by bringing to God a slain animal, that he deserved to be slain because of his sin. He who condemned himself was acquitted and accepted by God; while the other, who thought he acquitted himself so well was condemned to his confusion. The one thing which aggravated Cain's offence was, that when he found he was not right he would not accept God's way to be made right. God said to him, "If thou doest not well sin lieth at the door." At first sight it looks as if sin, like a wild beast, was crouching before him ready to spring upon him, but the better reading, as Rotherham renders it, is—"But if thou do not right, at the entrance a sin-bearer is lying." The sin-bearer, the animal for sacrifice, is rejected by Cain, and he is rejected by God in consequence. Anything that evolves from the earth-curse of our humanity cannot be admissible for salvation in any way, but Christ in His atoning death is admissible for salvation alway. The spotless Sin-Offering brought by the sinner not only avails for his pardon and acceptance, but makes him like the spotless victim, as assured by God's voice of love—"Thou art all fair, My love, there is no spot in thee."

THE CONSTRUCTED ARK AND THE SHELTERED
FAMILY (Genesis vi. 14)

Before the ark could be constructed, the wood from which it was made had to be cut down. The sheltering ark was made by the taking away of the life of the living tree. There are two passages where it was predicted that Christ would be "cut off." The first is in Isaiah liii. 8—"He was *cut off* out of the land of the living, for the transgression of My people was He stricken." The word *"cut off"* denotes exclusion or division. It is rendered *"divide"* when Solomon directed that the living child should be divided between the disputing mothers (1. Kings iii. 25, 26). The second Scripture is Daniel ix. 26, where we are told Messiah should be *"cut off."* The word means to be consumed, to be in want, and is rendered *"feller"* and *"cutteth"* in Jeremiah x. 3, in calling attention to the cutting down of trees, and the one who cut them down. The word is frequently employed in the Book of Leviticus in expressing God's judicial act in cutting off those who broke His law (Lev. vii. 20, 25, 27, &c.). Christ was cut off out of the land of the living, that we who had cut ourselves off from God by our sin, might be brought into the land of the living. He is the shelter for us from God's judgment, because there was no shelter for Him from it. He was excluded and separated from life, that we might be included and sanctified in the life which is the "life indeed." The exclusion and banishment of the Cross were for Him, and the inclusion and the blessing of God's throne are for us.

THE OFFERED SON AND THE PROVIDED
SUBSTITUTE (Genesis xxii. 1-14)

In Isaac being bound and in figure being surrendered to death, we have a type of Christ given over to our death (Hebrews xi. 19). God did not spare Himself, as He spared Abraham, from killing His Son. Isaac is seen going with Abraham to be offered up, bearing the wood on his shoulder, and with him and it are also associated the knife, the fire, and the binding upon the altar. On the Cross of Calvary we behold Christ offering Himself on the altar of His Deity, bearing the wood of our iniquity, the knife of justice entering the soul of His humanity, consumed by the fire of God's holy requirement, and the cords of love binding Him, through it all, to the altar of His voluntary sacrifice.

In the ram offered up in the stead of Isaac we have a type of God's provision for us. The word rendered *"stead of"* (verse 13) signifies, on behalf of. Dr. James Strong says, *"Tachath* means *'in lieu of,'* which is derived from *Towach*—to humble, depress." The usage of *"tachath"* suggests the thought of substitution, thus Seth is given *"instead"* of Abel (Genesis iv. 25); the man who injured the eye of his slave, so that he lost the use of it, had to let him go free *"for* his eye's sake" (Exodus xxi. 26); the stones taken out of the leprous house were changed for others which were put *"in the place"* of them (Leviticus xiv. 42); and David promised Amasa that he should be

captain *"in the room"* of Joab (II. Samuel xix. 13). As
we apply these illustrations of the use of the word, in
thinking of Christ as our Substitute, we exclaim in the language of Diognetus, who lived in the First Century, "God
Himself gave up His Son as a Ransom for us; the Holy
for the unholy; the Sinless for the sinful; the Immortal
for the mortal; for what but His righteousness could cover
our sins? O sweet change! O unsearchable work! O
unexampled benefit, that the wickedness of many should
be covered by the One righteous, the righteousness of One
should justify many sinners!"

THE ERECTED ALTARS AND THEIR TEACHING

The altar is symbolical of communion with the Lord on
the ground of sacrifice. Dr James Strong, in his Hebrew
lexicon, in explaining the word rendered altar, says, *"Miz-
beach,* from *Zabach,* a primary root, to slaughter an animal,
usually in sacrifice." *Zabach* is rendered in the margin of
Gen. xxxi. 54, *"killed,"* and *"offered"* in Gen. xlvi. 1.
"Altar" is mentioned thirteen times in the Book of Genesis,
and in connection with the following thoughts—

Satisfaction to God (viii. 20).
Promise from Him (xii. 7).
Remembrance of Him (xii. 8).
Restoration in Him (xiii. 4).
Fellowship with Him (xiii. 18).
Obedience to Him (xxii. 9).
Prayer to Him (xxvi. 25).
Claiming for Him (xxxiii. 20).
Consecration to Him (xxxv. 1, 3, 7).

All this emphasises and typifies that Christ in His atonement brings God to us in blessing, and brings us to Him

in fellowship. A bloodless altar brings a curse upon the offerer, while a blood-atoning altar is the mystic power, which, like the magic wand and the cave of legend, silvers everything with blessing.

THE SUFFERINGS AND THE GLORY OF JOSEPH

The history of Joseph is briefly summarised in Psalm cv. 18-22. There is no man who stands out in such moral beauty as Joseph in the whole of the sacred writings, and who is such a perfect type of Christ. His career flashes out with typical references to Christ. I only note two in connection with the words, "His feet they hurt with fetters, his soul came into iron" (margin, R.V., verse 18); and "He made him lord of his house, and ruler of all his substance" (verse 21). The iron of suffering entered into the soul of Christ before He entered into the sphere of supremacy. The visit of His humiliation and the prison of His crucifixion were the preludes to the position of honour. He suffered outside the camp as our Sin-Bearer, and now we stand inside the vail with Him. He endured our prison-death, that we might enjoy with Him His palace-life. Being in the exalted place, because He passed through the expiating one, He now says, "I was dead and am alive for evermore"; and we can say, too, "I was dead, and in Christ, I am alive for evermore."

II. *The Atoning Saviour in the Psalms*

There are three Psalms which are specially Calvary's ones, namely, Psalms xxii., xxxviii., and lxix. Let us look at a few sentences in the first of these. The title of Psalm xxii. is striking—"the hind of the morning or dawn."

Delitzsch remarks, according to the traditional definition, it refers "to the early light preceding the dawn of the morning, whose first rays are likened to the horns of the hind." It is not without meaning, too, that the lamb of the morning sacrifice was offered up as the watchman cried out, "The first rays of the morning burst forth." The light of grace flashes forth from the darkness of the cross. The hind that was stricken in death is the one who brings life to us.

THE FORSAKEN SURETY

"My God, My God, why hast Thou forsaken Me?" (verse 1). He that standeth Surety for another shall smart for it. Man had forsaken God, the Fountain of Living Waters (Jer. ii. 13), and he must answer for his sin, or another must answer for him. Christ came to us where we were, and answered for us in standing as our Surety. He was forsaken by the Righteous God as He bore the penalty of our sin. The word *"forsaken"* is rendered *"left destitute"* in Genesis xxiv. 27; and *"faileth"* in Psalm xxxviii. 10. These words might be read into the text, and as they are, they give added emphasis to the fact that Christ was left alone, He was destitute of help, Heaven failed Him, and God forsook Him. When Martin Luther was confronted with this fact, he sat benumbed for a time, and exclaimed at last, "God forsaken by God." He was destitute of help that we might have salvation. He was failed in the hour of His extremity that God might never fail us in any extremity. He was forsaken that the blood-bought promise might be ours—"I will never leave thee nor forsake thee." He was orphaned that we might be Fathered.

"THE LOWLY WORM" (verse 6)

The worm means a maggot. The word *"tolaath"* applies especially to the coccus, from which the scarlet dye was obtained to dye the scarlet things of the tabernacle. The death of the worm was necessary to get the dye. There are two very significant occurrences of the word *"scarlet."* One is in Isaiah i. 18, where man's sins are said to be "as *scarlet,"* and the other is, when reference is made to the *"scarlet"* used in the different curtains and vail of the tabernacle (Exodus xxvi. 1). Christ, in calling Himself *"a Worm,"* identifies Himself with the uncleanness of man's sin, and the heinousness of his iniquity; and the scarlet being associated with the dwelling-place of Jehovah, which was typical of Christ tabernacling among us, suggests the thought that He became our sin that we might become God's sanctuary. The worm Jacob is no longer a worm but a son of God, because the Son of God became as a worm. The scarlet dye of His blood makes us fit to become the dwelling-place of God. Christ said, "I am . . . no Ish" (*"Ish"* is the word for man of high degree, as *"enosh"* refers to man as a poor, frail, incurable creature). He became so low that He repudiates the title to manhood in its highest form, to which He alone was entitled. Why? The reason is, He became lower than the lowest, that He might save the vilest, and lift up to the highest dignity and blessedness.

THE REPROACHED REDEEMER

"A reproach of men" (verse 6). The word *"reproach"* comes from a root which means to pull off, to strip, to expose to shame. The word is used in this sense when God says to Israel, "Thy shame shall be seen" (Isaiah xlvii.

3), and when the wicked shall awake "to *shame* and ever-lasting contempt" (Dan. xii. 2). Why did Christ submit to the shame of the cross? The answer is given by Christ Himself in another Psalm, where He says, "The zeal of Thine house hath eaten Me up: and the reproaches of them that reproached Thee have fallen upon Me" (Psalm lxix. 9). The result is, as the reproach of Egypt was rolled away from Israel at Gilgal (Josh. v. 9), so the reproach of sin has fallen upon Him on our account, and there is now no reproach for us. It is rolled away from us, because it was rolled over upon Him. He was shamed that we might not be put to shame.

> "Bearing shame and scoffing rude,
>
> In my place condemned He stood."

THE WEAKENED SAVIOUR

"I am *poured out,*" &c. (verse 14). The wise woman of Tekoah said that man in the frailty of his humanity was like "water spilt on the ground" (11. Samuel xiv. 14); and when Belshazzar came face to face with the hand of judgment writing his doom upon the wall, it is said, "the joints of his loins were loosed" (Daniel v. 6). *"Without strength"* (Romans v. 6) are the Spirit-inspired words which declare the inability of man; and surely it is with Divine intent that the Holy Spirit uses the very same expression in describing the sufferings of Christ, when He says He was "crucified through *weakness*" (11 Cor. xiii. 4). He has accomplished more in His weakness than others have done in the greatness of their strength. His impotency in death has brought to us the omnipotence of His life.

THE WITHERED SUFFERER

The intensity of His suffering is more pronounced as He suffers on. "My strength is *dried up* like a potsherd" (verse 15). One of the things which impresses the student is, the very words which describe the sinfulness and helplessness of the sinner are applied to the suffering Saviour. The word rendered *"dried up"* (*"Jabesh"*) means to be confused, to be dried up like water in a brook, or to be withered up like herbage. It is rendered *"withereth"* in Psalm xc. 6, in speaking of the frailty of man; *"dried up,"* in comparing Ephraim to a smitten tree (Hos. ix. 16); *"dried up,"* in describing the effect of the judgment of God upon Jeroboam when his hand was paralysed (1. Kings xiii. 4); and when the Psalmist was made conscious of his sin, he said, "My heart is smitten and *withered* like grass" (Psalm cii. 4). All this, when read in the light of Calvary, proclaims Christ's utter exhaustion, and reminds us of His cry, "I thirst." He came into our frailty that we might have His vitality. He was like a smitten tree, that He might make us living trees, full of the sap of His life. Death held Him in its paralysing grip, that Christ might hold us in His powerful grace; He was like a dried-up brook, that He might be to us the Water of Life; and He cried, "I thirst," that we might never cry for a drop of water in hell to cool our parched tongue.

I have only indicated the trend of this substitutionary Psalm, but as the whole of it is pondered we are made conscious that Christ is declaring the inmost heart of His experience. This Psalm reveals Christ as the Sin-Offering, as the Fortieth Psalm unfolds Him as the Burnt-Offering. He suffers alone. None can help. In His forsaking we have our welcome. In His death He gives us His life. In His emptying we receive His fulness.

III. *The Atoning Saviour in the Prophets.* There are many passages in the Prophets which are indicative and typical of Christ's death. Jeremiah in his sorrow (Lam. i. 12), Ezekiel's sacrificial waters (Ezek. xlvii. 1), Jonah in the place of death (Jonah ii. 6), Hosea's door of hope (Hosea ii. 15), Joel's Zion of deliverance (Joel ii. 32), Micah's kinsman Redeemer (Micah iv. 10), Nahum's publisher of peace (Nahum i. 15), Habakkuk's "bright beams out of his side" (Hab. iii. 4, margin), Zephaniah's just Lord (Zephaniah iii. 5), Haggai's "Desire of all nations" (Hag. ii. 7), Zechariah's pierced Friend, and smitten Shepherd (Zechariah xiii. 6, 7), and Malachi's Messenger of the Covenant (Malachi iii. 1). I call attention to only one, namely, the Smitten Shepherd.

THE SMITTEN SHEPHERD

"Awake, O sword, against My Shepherd, and against the Man that is My Fellow, saith the Lord of Hosts, smite the Shepherd" (Zech. xiii. 7). Let us look at Christ as the Smitten Shepherd. The word, to smite, occurs more than once in connection with Christ. Christ uses it in prophecy when He says, "I gave My back to the smiters" (Isaiah l. 6), and "I was *wounded* in the house of My friends" (Zech. xiii. 6), and when He was esteemed to be *"smitten* of God and afflicted" (Isa. liii. 4). Frequently the word is used to designate God's act of judgment. For instance, when the Lord *"smote* the firstborn of Egypt" (Exodus xii. 29), and when the angel of the Lord *smote* the Assyrians (Isaiah xxxvii. 36).

One has said, "Not to realise hell is not to prize the cross." Those who realise the hell of their sin's deserving are quick to recognise the sufficiency and suitability of the Saviour's substitution. The sin-burdened soul knows he has placed himself, by his sin, under the smiting of God's wrath, but he is ready also to appreciate the fact that Christ has been stricken on his behalf. His smiting is our salvation.

While passing the World's Fair at St. Louis, on the night train, in 1904, the whole scene was one mass of magnificent electric light. As I was admiring the flashing display of the lights on the Festal Hall, the lights upon it suddenly changed to a deep crimson, which made everything seem warm with their hue. Amid all the wonders of God's creation, the works of His historic and providential hand, and the certainty of the Festal Hall of His Word, there is one crimson fact which illuminates the whole, and that is the atoning sacrifice of Christ's death. Vinet has tersely put the whole issue so far as Christianity is concerned. He says, "Deprived of the great fact of expiation, what, I ask, is Christianity? For ordinary minds, an ordinary morality; for others, an abyss of inconsistencies." With the "great fact of expiation," what does Christianity proclaim? It proclaims *the bow of God's love* in the dark cloud of sin, telling us that judgment is past (Genesis ix. 13; Rev. iv. 3; v. 9); it proclaims *the token of assurance* in the dark night of wrath, which assures us that the plague of indignation shall not come near us (Exodus xii. 13; Rom. viii. 1-3); it proclaims that *the ransom price of redemption* has been paid for us, thus counting us in God's elect (Exodus xxx. 12-14; 1. Peter i. 18, 19); it proclaims *the solid foundation of atonement* on which we rest, and with which we are identified (Exodus xxxviii. 25-28; 1. Corinthians iii. 11); it proclaims *the uplifted serpent of life-bestowment*, bringing life and health and the sun-rising of expectant outlook (Numbers xxi. 8, 9; John iii. 14, 15); it proclaims *the ashes of the red-heifer of*

cleansing from defilement and restoration to fellowship
(Numbers xix. 1-14; 1. John i. 7); and it proclaims *the
consecrating ram of holiness* bringing us untold blessing,
and qualifying us for God's priestly service (Leviticus viii.
22-29; Hebrews xiii. 12).

The supreme attraction, yea, the attraction of God's
Word, is the One of Whom the late Charles Fox wrote:

"Marred more than any man's, yet there is no place
In this wide universe but gains new grace,
Richer and fuller, from that marred face."

5

God and Christ's Atonement

There are two ways by which the Niagara Falls may be reached. They may be reached from the Atlantic Ocean, by going up the St. Lawrence, past the Thousand Islands, across Lake Ontario, up the Niagara river, past the whirlpool, and through the rapids. The other way to reach the Falls is to start from the Rocky Mountains, and go through the four lakes, Superior, Michigan, Huron, and Erie, which are the feeders of the Falls. As we look at Christ in His atonement, we may view Him from two standpoints. We may view the ocean of God's love as it touches us in our necessity, the St. Lawrence of His grace, the thousand and more blessings the Lord bestows, the lake of the calm peace with God, and the whirlpool and rapids of His power, and we apprehend they all come to us from the pains of the Niagara of Christ's death. Or we may view the atoning death of Christ from God's standpoint, and start from the Rockies of God's eternal purpose, and trace the wondrous path of Christ's obedience unto death as revealed in the four mighty lakes of the four gospels, and see the mighty display of the deep of God's love calling to the deep of His righteousness as they crash and flow at the Niagara of Christ's death.

I purpose to call attention to Christ's death from the latter standpoint, as the display of God's provision. The vastness of this section of the topic compels me to confine myself to one section of God's Word, namely, the Epistle to the Romans.

I.—GOD'S PURPOSE IN CHRIST'S DEATH

"Whom God hath set forth to be a propitiation through faith, by His blood" (Rom. iii. 25, R. v.). The words, "By His Blood," as Bishop Ellicott remarks, are to be associated with "Whom God hath set forth to be a propitiation." He renders the words, "Whom God hath set forth by the shedding of His blood to be a propitiatory offering through faith." And he comments, "It was in the shedding of the blood that the essence of the atonement exhibited upon the cross consisted. No doubt other portions of the life of Christ led up to this one, but this was the culminating act in it, viewed as an atonement."

God is here viewed as One Who is an Exhibitor, or the cross is the culmination of a specific purpose from which flashes out unmistakable truth, like the flashing forth of an electric light in the lighthouse across the foaming waves. The electricity which illuminated the lamp was there before the current was switched on, but it was set forth by the switching on. The word *"set forth"* signifies to set before one's self, that is an inward purpose. The compound word occurs in two other places. Paul uses it when he writes to the saints at Rome, and says, "I *purposed* to come to you" (Romans i. 13); and it is used of God's loving purpose and will, when the apostle says, He made known to us "the mystery of His will, according to His good pleasure which he hath *purposed* in Himself" (Ephesians i. 9). The death of Christ was the unfolding of the secret purpose of God. Moule finely says, "Here is no fortuitous concourse, but the long-laid plan of God. Behold its procuring cause, magnificent, tender, Divine, human, spiritual, historic. It is the Beloved Son of the Father; no antagonist power from a region alien to the blessed law and its Giver. The Law-Giver is the Christ-Giver; He has *'set Him forth.'*

He has provided in Him an expiation which—does not persuade Him to have mercy . . . but liberates His love along the line of a wonderfully satisfied holiness."

II.—GOD'S COMMENDATION OF HIS LOVE IN CHRIST'S DEATH

"God commendeth His love towards us, in that, while we were yet sinners Christ died for us" (Romans v. 8). One has said of the word *"commendeth,"* it means "to place together; of persons to introduce to one's acquaintance and favourable notice, hence, to commend, to represent as worthy." The word is translated *"stood with"* in calling attention to the fact that Moses and Elijah were with Christ on the Mount of Transfiguration (Luke ix. 32). It is rendered *"make"* in recording what Paul said, when he declared he would "make" himself a transgressor if he went back to the law after having accepted the gospel (Galatians ii. 18). Very often the word is used in the sense of approving another in commending to some one's favourable notice (Rom. xvi. 1, 2; 11. Corinthians vii. 11; x. 18). The sense in each case is one person being so identified with another that they stand together, just as David assured Abiathar his life was safe as long as he abode with him (1. Samuel xxii. 23). God associates Himself in His love with the death of Christ for sinners, and the striking point of contrast is, man may sacrifice himself for a good man, God sacrificed Himself for bad men— "sinners." The gospel is a glorious fact about an act. The act of Christ's death commends the fact of God's love. The arms of Christ's cross are the arms of Divine love. Some would have the cross without the blood, that is Ritualism; others have a Christ without His cross, that is Unitarianism; we have Christ with His cross, that is redemption, for in Him and it we find God Himself.

III.—GOD'S MISSION IN CHRIST'S DEATH

"God sending His own Son in the likeness of sinful flesh" (Romans viii. 3). Dr. Denney says, "It is the atonement which explains the incarnation. The incarnation takes place in order that the sin of the world may be put away by the offering of the body of Jesus Christ. The obedience of the Incarnate One, like all obedience has moral value—that is, it has a value for Himself; but its redemptive value, *i. e.,* its value for us belongs to it not simply as obedience, but as obedience to a will of God which requires the Redeemer to take upon Himself in death, the responsibility of the sin of the world."

The incarnation of Christ among us does not explain His substitution for us, but His substitution for us explains His incarnation among us, even as the coal from the pit explains the necessity of sinking the shaft. As the shaft is the means to get at the coal, and thus demonstrates its purpose, so the end of the incarnation, His substutionary sacrifice, proves the necessity of the means to that end, namely, that He should become a man to die for men.

As locating the origin of the provision which God Himself has made, the word "sending" indicates not the object to which one is sent, but the sender who commissions; thus the thought is, not sending to, but sending from—a letting go. There is a stronger word than "pempo," namely, "apostello," which signifies, not merely a letting go, but to send forth one on a mission and fully equip him for it; thus apostello implies the mission he has to fulfil, and the authority which backs him. Both words are used of Christ, especially in John's Gospel.

"Pempo" occurs twenty-five times (John iv. 34; v. 23,

24. 30, 37; vi. 38, 39, 40, 44; vii. 16, 18, 28, 33; viii. 16, 18, 26, 29; ix. 4; xii. 44, 45, 49; xiii. 20; xiv. 24; xv. 21; xvi. 5); and *"apostello"* occurs seventeen times (John iii. 17, 34; v. 36, 38; vi. 29, 57; vii. 29; viii. 42; x. 36; xi. 42; xvii. 3, 8, 18, 21, 23, 25; xx. 21). The word in Rom viii. 3 signifies merely a letting go, but the word in John iii. 17 signifies a fitting out for His mission. So taken together, God sent Him, that is, let Him go, to be condemned for us, but He did not equip Him to condemn, but to save us.

IV.—GOD DEALING WITH SIN IN CHRIST'S DEATH

"By a sacrifice for sin condemned sin in the flesh" (Romans viii. 3, margin). In a general way, by the holiness of His nature, God must condemn sin; but the statement before us says He condemned sin in a *specific* way, that is, He judged Christ for us. The expression, "for sin," takes us back to the Old Testament, especially to the Book of Leviticus, where the words for *"sin"* and *"sin-offering,"* which are the same, occur over seventy times. The words *"for sin"* and *"for a sin-offering"* occur twenty-eight times In one chapter, the chapter of the sin-offering (Leviticus iv.) the words occur nine times (Leviticus iv. 3, 8, 14, 20, 28, 32, 33, 35). The typical significance of sin and sin-offering being one and the same, identifies the sin with the offering, and the offering with the sin. Christ identified Himself with the believer's sin, and the believer is identified with Christ, Who gave Himself as an offering for sin, so that in Him the believer has answered for his sin, and has been judged for it. Luther tersely put it—"He is my sin and I am His righteousness"; or, as Hooker remarks, "We have no knowledge in the world but this, that man hath sinned and God has suffered; that God made Himself the sin of men that men might be made the righteousness of God."

The force and forcefulness of the word *"condemned"* must not be overlooked. It embraces the three thoughts, a crime committed, a verdict passed, and a punishment meted out. Take two illustrations. Noah's act in building the ark is said to be not only a means of salvation to his house, but that "by which he condemned the world" (Hebrews xi. 7); and of God's act of judgment upon Sodom it is said to have been *condemned* with an overthrow ((II. Peter ii. 6). In each case there is the sin which called forth the sentence of judgment and the execution of the judgment in the subsequent condemnation. In Christ's unjust condemnation there are the same three things. He was charged with the crime of blasphemy, and the consequence was "they all *condemned* Him to be guilty of death" (Mark xiv. 64). As God condemned the old world by the flood of judgment, and the cities of the plain by the baptism of fire; so He condemned His Son for us. Can we not imagine an Israelite as he stood watching the fire feeding upon the sin-offering till it was wholly consumed, saying "There am I dying for my sin, bearing the wrath of God against it?"

V.—GOD NOT SPARING HIS SON FROM DEATH

"He spared not His own Son" (Romans viii. 32). Some expressions of the Bible touch a cord which recalls many incidents, such is the expression "spared not," it links our thought to Divine prohibition and incident. Jehovah's injunction to Moses regarding the idolator was that he was not to be spared from being put to death (Deut. xiii. 6-9; xxix. 20); the sin of Saul was that he dared to spare Agag and the goodly of the cattle, when God told him to utterly destroy and not to spare (1. Samuel xv. 3, 9); Jehovah did not spare the Egyptians from death when Pharaoh and his people dared to oppose Him (Psalm lxxviii. 50); He did not spare the angels from hell and the chains of darkness when they rebelled against Him (ii. Pet. ii. 4); He did not spare the antediluvians from judgment who were disobedient to His warning voice (ii. Peter ii. 5); Jehovah did not spare the nation of Israel from being cut off from blessing when in unbelief they forsook Him (Romans xi. 21); and He did not spare Himself, although He had said a father always spares the son who serves him (Malachi iii. 17), from smiting His Son when He gave Him to be our Substitute. Why did He not spare Him? If we are to be spared He must not be spared. Sodom and Gomorrah would have been spared for the sake of ten righteous men (Genesis xviii. 24, &c.), we are spared for the sake of the One, Who was bruised by Jehovah, and because His stroke fell on Him (Isaiah liii. 8, 10).

VI.—GOD GIVING UP CHRIST TO DEATH

"Delivered Him up for us all" (Romans viii. 32). When Henry Martin reached the shores of India he made this entry in his journal—"I desire to burn out for my God." From whence did he get this flame of burning desire? It was from the sacred fire of God's heart of love as seen flaming on the cross of Christ's passion. One of the strongest words is used to describe God's act of love when it says, *"He delivered up."* The Greek word means to give over into the hands of another. It is translated *"gave up"* and *"gave over"* in describing God's act of giving over to sin and its consequences, those who had previously given themselves over to sin (Romans i. 24, 26, 28; Ephesians iv. 19), and the word is also translated *"given"* and *"gave"* and *"committed"* in speaking of

Christ's act in giving Himself up to death on our account (Galatians ii. 20; Ephesians v. 2, 25), and in His committing Himself to His Father (1. Pet. ii. 23). We are not left in any doubt as to the reason of this giving up, for we are distinctly told He "was *delivered up* for our trespasses" (Romans iv. 25, R.V.). One of the most intense and soul-anguishing cries of the Bible is that of David for Absalom—"My son, my son Absalom! would God I had died for thee, O Absalom, my son, my son!" (11. Samuel xviii. 33). From a very different cause it seems some such feeling must have been in the heart of Jehovah when He gave up the worthy Son of His love for the worthless sons of men.

VII.—GOD FOR US IN THE DEATH OF HIS SON

There are seven wonderful questions brought out in Romans viii. 31-35, which are prefaced by one general question, that is, if we take the English Revised Version. Rotherham makes the questions ten. Perhaps the better way will be to take the Authorised, and compare it with Rotherham's translation:

AUTHORIZED	ROTHERHAM
1. What shall we then say to these things?	1. What then shall we say to these things?
2. If God be for us, who can be against us?	2. If God is for us, who shall be against us?
3. He that spared not His own Son, but delivered Him up for us all, how shall He not with Him also freely give us all things?	3. He at least, Who His own Son did not spare, but in behalf of us all delivered Him up, how shall He not also with Him all things upon us in favour bestow?
4. Who shall lay anything to the charge of God's elect?	4. Who shall bring an accusation against the chosen ones of God?

5. *It is* God that justifieth.

5. God Who declareth righteous?

6. Who is he that condemneth?

6. Who is he that condemneth?

7. *It is* Christ that died, yea, rather, that is risen again, Who is even at the right hand of God, Who also maketh intercession for us.

7. Christ Jesus Who died? Nay, rather was raised from among the dead, Who is on the right hand of God, Who also is making intercession on our behalf?

8. Who shall separate us from the love of Christ?

8. Who shall separate us from the love of the Christ?

It will be noted that points five and seven in the Authorised Version make the Apostle give a definite statement, whereas Rotherham makes him ask a series of questions. I am inclined to believe that the latter is the correct way to look at the passage, as the margin of the Revised Version also suggests. God, Who has declared the believer righteous, will certainly not bring an accusation against us, and Christ, Who died and is risen, will not condemn us, for He died and rose again to free us from condemnation, and He also lives to meet any who would condemn us.

The death of Christ proclaims God's gift of Christ to act for us, and He gives to God what meets God's righteous requirement, and Christ in turn meets our need. Thus all Christ gave and did, are the giving, and the doing of God Himself.

All this brings out the fact that the crowning act of Revelation is the mighty act of God's love in the death of His Son. "Herein is love," is the comment of the Holy Spirit, "not that we loved God, but that He loved us, and sent His Son to be the Propitiation for our sins" (1. John iv. 10).

Hatton, in *Cruel London*, represents two of his characters standing at the door of their dwelling-place on Christmas Day. "Kerman went to the door. The snow had ceased to fall. The sun was getting up behind them. A grey mist brooded over the vast expanse of hill and dale. The sun seemed to dwell upon it. A fog-bow appeared in the sky; and beneath it the form of a cross.

" 'Come here, Decker, quick!' cried Kerman.

"Decker hurried to the door.

" 'What's that?'

" 'A phenomenon peculiar to mountainous countries. It is common in the Arctic regions and in the Alps. In the Hartz they are spectres. But I've never seen the figure of a cross before.'

"As he spoke the phenomenon disappeared. Kerman looked anxiously at Decker—'What's the meaning of it?'

" 'It's an omen.'

" 'Of what?'

" 'That God will not desert us. It is Christmas Day. He sends us His great sign manual, the cross of Christ.'

"The face of the American lighted up, as he spoke, with a sublime expression of tenderness and hope.

"Kerman bent his head reverently.

" 'Let us go in, Jack, and pray. Don't let us be ashamed of our feelings; don't let us be afraid to speak to God in each other's hearing. We shall want His aid before long. Your shovel is no good against a tempest of wind.' "

The incident proclaims the inspiration and encouragement which the cross of Christ brings, as expressing the love of God for man. In the light of the cross every darkness is dispelled, every sin killed, every question answered, every foe dispelled, every fear quenched, every hunger satisfied, every hope met, every longing fulfilled, and **every promise kept.**

6

Sin and Christ's Atonement

Low thoughts about sin will lead to lower thoughts about Christ's sacrifice. He who only sees a man suffering in a good cause in the Christ of Calvary fails to understand the teaching of Scripture. The Spirit's utterance is clear and emphatic as to Christ's death in relation to sin and sinners.

Let us put the whole subject in the form of questions.

1. *For whom did Christ die?*

Christ is said to have died for "sinners" and for the "ungodly," and that God's "enemies" are reconciled to Him by the death of His Son (Romans v. 6, 8, 10).

2. *For what did He die?*

"Our sins"—"He died for our sins according to the Scriptures" (1. Cor. xv. 3).

3. *Why did Christ come into the world?*

To "put away sin by the sacrifice of Himself (Hebrews ix. 26). "He was manifested to take away our sins" (1. John iii. 5).

4. *Did God have anything to do with that death for sin?*

He made "His soul an offering for sin" (Isaiah liii. 10). "He made Him to be sin for us" (11. Cor. v. 21).

"God sending His Son . . . by a sacrifice for sin, condemned sin in the flesh" (Rom. viii. 3, margin).

5. *Did Christ die willingly?*

"He gave Himself for our sins" (Gal. i. 4).

6. *What did He do with our sins?*

"Bare the sins of many" (Isaiah liii. 12).

"Offered to bear the sins of many" (Heb. ix. 28).

7. *Where did He bear our sins?*

"In His own body on the tree" (1. Peter ii. 24).

8. *Is it necessary for Him to repeat the act?*

"Christ died (R. V., margin) for sins once" (1. Peter iii. 18).

Offering of the body of Jesus Christ once for all (Hebrews x. 12).

9. *Why did He die?*

To make an atonement for sin (Heb. i. 3; ii. 17, R. V.; 1. John ii. 2).

To put away the hindrance of sin (Heb. ix. 26).

To take away the guilt of sin (Rom. iv. 25).

To cleanse from the pollution of sin (Rev. i. 5).

To make us dead to sins (1. Peter ii. 24).

To constitute us righteous (Rom. v. 19, R. V.; 11. Corinthians v. 21).

To deliver us from the world (Gal. i. 4).

To separate us from self (11. Cor. v. 14, 15).

To bring us to God (1. Peter iii. 18).

I have only called attention to a few of the Scriptures where Christ's death is directly associated with sin. The one thing I want to emphasize is this, that the very words which are used to describe man's sin are found connected directly or indirectly with Christ's sacrifice for sin: showing His identification with it, and His complete answer to God for it.

Let us look at some Old Testament words.

I.—SIN

The principal word for sin is to miss the mark. Of the left-handed Benjaminites it is said, they "could sling a stone at a hair-breadth and not *miss*" (Judges xx. 16). The word to *"miss"* is rendered sin again and again. Saul, for instance, confesses, "I have *sinned*" (1. Samuel xv. 24). He had deviated from the express command of God to slay all that pertained to Amalek. He missed his step and fell to his hurt. Canon Girdlestone calls attention to the fact that the same word is found in connection with the offerings for sin and the blessings which accrue. "The Piel form, or intensive voice, of this verb is rendered as follows: *to make reconciliation* (11. Chronicles xxix. 24); *to bear loss* (Genesis xxxi. 39); *offered it for sin* (Lev. ix. 15); to *cleanse from sin* (Ex. xxix. 36); and *to purge* or *purify* (Lev. viii. 15)."

The sin offering is a type of Christ as the One Who has borne the judgment of God against sin. All the offering that was burnt outside the camp was utterly consumed (Lev. iv. 11, 12). The sinner deserves to be consumed with the judgment of God because of his sin. As the offerer watched the burning of the victim, he would say, "There am I, and my sin being consumed in the offering offered in my stead."

Christ has so identified Himself with our sin that He speaks of it as His own, hence, in the prophetic word we hear Him saying, "There is no rest in My bones, because of My sin" (Psalm xxxviii. 3). The rest, the peace, the health (see margin), which come to us, are because there were no rest and peace for Him. "Because of my sin, He died," the believer says, and because He said "my sin," in taking our place, we shall not be called upon to answer for it again, for in Him it is answered for already.

The word for sin is rendered *"bare the loss"* in Genesis xxxi. 39, when Jacob recounts to Laban what he had done in his service. "That which was torn of beasts I brought not unto thee; I bare the loss of it . . . in the day the drought consumed me, and the frost by night, ana my sleep departed from mine eyes." Sleepless, cold, and consumed Jacob said he was in Laban's service, and bore loss too. How much fuller and deeper these words describe what our Lord endured for us. He was chilled by the affronts of man, scorched by the judgment of God, and lost all the bliss of heaven for the time being, to save us from the bitterness of hell and to bring us into the blessedness of heaven.

II.—INIQUITY

The Hebrew word *"avah"* means a distortion, as when a person's body is distorted because he is in pain, or a woman in travail. It is rendered *"bowed down"* in Isaiah xxi. 3. It means also to pervert, as when one goes astray from the right path, hence, it is rendered *"perverted"* in calling attention to Israel's forgetting the Lord (Jer. iii. 21). Its full significance, as descriptive of sin, is to do wrong or wickedly, hence, it corresponds to our word *"wrong,"* namely, that which is wrung out of its course. (See the word rendered *"done wickedly"* in II. Sam. xxiv. 17; *"done perversely"* in I. Kings viii. 47; *"done amiss"* in II. Chronicles vi. 37; and *"committed iniquity"* in Psalm cvi. 6).

Christ in the prophetic Psalm of His suffering says, "I am *troubled"* (Ps: xxxviii. 6). . The word *"troubled"* or *"bent"* is the same as rendered *"iniquity."* We had bent ourselves by sin, and perverted the powers which God had entrusted to us for His glory to our own use. Christ had to be bent in suffering for us before we could be righted and brought back to the right path. Sin had overturned everything (the word is rendered *"overturn"* in Ezekiel xxi. 27), and Christ came into our ruin that He might turn us again, and make us to be as we were. Dr. Maclaren renders the sentence, "I am twisted with pain," and comments, "Contorted in pain, bent down by weakness . . . burning with inward fever, diseased in every tortured atom of flesh, He is utterly worn out and broken." The intensity of the Lord's sufferings can only be measured by the holiness of God, by the righteousness of the law, by the desert of sin, by the pangs of death, by the woes of the lost, and by the pains of hell.

III.—TRANSGRESSION

Transgression is the passing over the boundary of God's law. Man in his self-will daring to *"go beyond"* (word rendered *"go beyond"* in Numbers xxii. 18) the prohibition of Jehovah, hence, Saul *"transgressed* the commandment of the Lord" (1. Samuel xv. 24), and Israel *"transgressed* the covenant" (Hosea vi. 7; viii. 1). The word, in a general way, means to pass over or to pass by, as a lamp passing between two objects (Gen. xv. 17) ; as a person passing over a river (Deuteronomy xii. 10) ; and as waves passing over an individual to his submergence (Psalm cxxiv. 4, 5).

Christ uses the word in this latter sense when He realizes the waves of God's wrath against sin are submerging Him, and as identified with our sins, says, "Mine iniquities are *gone over* Mine head" (Psalm xxxviii. 4). Jonah passed over the command of the Lord and had to bear the punishment of his disobedience, as he says, "Thy waves *passed over* me" (Jonah ii. 3) ; so we have transgressed God's law, and we deserve to be punished; but Christ, our Divine Jonah, has been plunged beneath the waters of judgment on our behalf, and now we can bear our testimony and say, "He hath made to meet upon Him the iniquity of us all."

IV.—REBELLION

To sin is bad, to distort the right and make it wrong is worse, to go beyond the Divine fiat is worst, but to add rebellion to these is worse than the worst. God said to Israel, "I have nourished and brought up children, and they have *rebelled* against Me" (Isa. i. 2). When one has failed to do right, done absolute wrong, broken the law, and then dares to stand with clenched fist and defy the One against Whom the previous acts had been committed, he deserves to be left for judgment. Did God thus leave the sinner? No. Here is the wonder of the Gospel. Four times the word rendered *"sin"* and *"rebelled"* is applied to Christ. It is translated in Isaiah liii. 5, 8, 12—*"Transgression"* and *"Transgressors."* Here, again, we are impressed with Christ's close identification with our sin, for the literal meaning of the sentence, "wounded for our *transgressions"* is, "He was the wounded One unto death because of our transgressions." As Newton says, literally, "from our transgressions. Our transgressions are here spoken of as the source whence the sufferings spoken of flowed out to our Substitute." This oneness with us and our oneness with Him is further emphasized in the words, "Numbered with the *transgressors."*

I remember a brother in reading the words of Scripture descriptive of Christ being crucified with the two thieves read it as follows: "Where they crucified Him, and two other malefactors with Him." By adding the word "other" the reader made Christ a malefactor. This could not be true personally, but it was true representatively, for being "numbered with the transgressors" (Mark xv. 28), He was treated as a thief (Mark xv. 28). Mark it does not say He was numbered with sinners, but with *"transgressors,"* namely, rebels. The full force is further brought out when it is known that the word *"malefactor"* means a doer of some particular evil. The two thieves suffered the just penalty of the law (Luke xxiii. 41), because of some particular crime. Christ identified Himself with the worst of characters that He might save the worst of them. The arms of the atoning Saviour are found beneath the lowest. His blood is sufficient to cleanse the vilest, and it is efficient to all who will receive Him.

V.—UNFAITHFULNESS, OR TRESPASS

The Hebrew word *"ma'al"* seems to indicate faithlessness, treachery, and apostasy. It is rendered *"trespass"* about thirty times. Parkhurst says of its meaning—"To straddle with the feet too much to one side, and so decline towards it . . . a declining or deflection from duty and truth." The word is rendered *"falsehood"* in Job xxi. 34. This word makes sin yet blacker. It is employed to describe the sin of Achan (Joshua vii. 1), for he was unfaithful to his trust in taking to his own use what Jehovah had consecrated to Himself. Under the law, if an Israelite sinned, committed a trespass against the Lord, ignorantly, in the holy things (Lev. v. 15, 16), or if he trespassed against the Lord in deceiving his neighbour (Lev. vi. 2-7), then he had to make amends according to the Lord's directions, but in each case there had to be a trespass-offering, by means of which the priest had to "make an atonement" for the offender, and then, when atonement was made, his trespass "shall be forgiven him" (Lev. v. 16; vi. 7). No atonement, no forgiveness.

While there is no direct statement about Christ dying for this sin, the typical significance of the trespass offering

and the priest making atonement by means of it, are sufficient to emphasize the New Testament statement, "In Whom
we have redemption through His blood, the forgiveness of
our *trespasses,* according to the riches of His grace"
(Ephesians i. 7, R. V.).

There is no more grievous sin than the five-fold apostasy
mentioned in Heb. vi. 4, 5, which culminates in crucifying
the Son of God afresh, and putting Him to an open shame;
and yet right in the midst of the solemn words there is the
grace of God held out to the penitent. It is impossible to
renew the unfaithful ones, *"So long* as they are again crucifying unto themselves the Son of God" (Rotherham's translation and footnote), but as soon as they repent they find
they are forgiven for the sake of Him Who made atonement
for sin.

VI.—OFFENCE, OR SINS OF OMISSION

The one sentence which sums up the meaning of the word
"trespassed" (Lev. v. 19), and which is rendered *"offend"*
(Hosea iv. 15), *"found faulty"* (Hosea x. 2), is, "Though
he wist it not, yet is he *guilty"* (Lev. v. 17). Ignorance
does not free the offender from guilt. The word is rendered
"trespass-offering" twenty-one times in the Book of Leviticus, and is translated *"sin"* in speaking of Christ being made
"an offering for *sin"* (Isaiah liii. 10). These words remind
us of the New Testament sentence, "He hath made Him to
be sin for us (II. Cor. v. 21). We cannot understand the
deep mystery of Christ being made sin for us, but we accept
its reality. Dr. Denney finely says, "It is a counsel of
despair to evade it. It is not the puzzle of the New Testament, but the ultimate solution of all puzzles; it is not an
irrational quantity that has to be eliminated or explained
away, but the keystone of the whole apostolic thought. It

is not a blank obscurity in revelation, a spot of impenetrable blackness. It is the focus in which the reconciling love of God burns with the purest and intensest flame; it is the foundation light of all day, the master light of all seeing, in the Christian revelation."

VII.—BURDEN

The Hebrew word *"'amal"* gives the consequence of sin, rather than its nature. It is rendered *"toil"* in Genesis xli. 51, *"perverseness"* in Numbers xxiii. 21, *"sorrow"* in Job iii. 10, *"wickedness"* in Job iv. 8, *"trouble"* in Job v. 7, *"miserable"* in Job xvi. 2, *"mischief"* in Psalm x. 7, *"pain"* in Psalm xxv. 18, *"labour"* and *"travail"* in Ecclesiastes i. 3; ii. 10, 11, 18, 19, 20, 21, 22, 24; and *"iniquity"* in Hab. i. 13. All this goes to show the toil and misery of sin; the pain it ministers to and the sorrow it causes. The word is applied to Christ in speaking of "the *travail* of His soul" (Isaiah liii. 11). Parkhurst says of the word, "Afflictive labour, toil, travail, weariness, irksomeness, which one endures oneself. Also what occasions toil or irksomeness to another, or, in our old English phrase, what irketh him."

When Joseph looked upon his firstborn, he called him Manasseh ("forgetting"); "for God," said he, "hath made me forget all my toil." He had been in the pit, and in the prison, and had been hurt (Psa. cv. 18), and misrepresented, but he forgot it all in the comfort of his home life; so Christ shall see the fruit of the "travail of His soul and be satisfied." Sin had caused us the travail and pain it always brings, and it brought Christ into pain and anguish, before He could bring us out of it. But since He has been into the place of sin's consequence and burden, He can bring out from sin's condemnation and curse.

7

Christ's and His Atonement

There were two large pillars at the entrance of the temple of Solomon, which were named Jachin and Boaz. The meanings of these names are suggestive. Jachin means "He will establish," and Boaz, "In Him is strength." There are two great pillars of truth at the entrance of the temple of Christ's teaching about His death, the understanding of which will establish us in salvation and sanctification, and give us strength in service, and these two truths are, the necessity and the nature of His atoning death.

Christ's Death: Its Necessity

Without going into the many-sidedness of the necessity of Christ's death, such as Justice demanded it (Eze. xviii. 4-9), Law required it (Gal. iii. 13), Sin called for it (Rom. iv. 25), Wrath is met by it (Rom. v. 9), Holiness is upheld by it (Rom. iii. 26), Mercy ministers because of it (Luke xxiv. 46, 47), Wisdom is displayed by it, Power is communicated through it (1. Cor. i. 24), and God is glorified by it (Eph. v. 2), I refer to Christ's own teaching about the necessity of His death.

There are three passages of Scripture in which Christ distinctly and definitely refers to the necessity of His death, and in these He is seen in the three characters of the Baptised Sufferer, the Dying Corn of Wheat, and the Uplifted Saviour.

1. The Baptised Sufferer.

"I have a baptism to be baptised with, and how am I

straitened till it be accomplished?" (Luke xii. 50). Rotherham translates the words, "But an immersion have I to be
immersed with, and how am I distressed till it be ended?"
Christ's baptism on the cross was symbolised by His baptism in Jordan.   There are three things we may ponder as
we take the one event as an illustration of the other. *When*
Christ was baptised, *where* He was baptised, and *who* baptised Him.

When was Christ baptised?   The skilled artist has no
superfluous touches in his painting.   He is not only guided
by the law of perspective, but by the law of unity; that is,
every touch has a relation to the picture as a whole.   The
same is true of the Holy Spirit as He depicts the Lord
Jesus in His baptism.   He says of Him, "Then cometh
Jesus from Galilee to Jordan unto John to be baptised of
him   (Matt. iii. 13).   That adverb of time *"Then"* is like a
red life-buoy upon a sea scene, it strikes the eye of medita-
tion at once.   What was John doing at the time?   Baptising
the people in Jordan upon the confession of their sins (Matt.
iii. 6).   But Christ had no sins to confess, therefore, John
was perfectly justified in refusing to baptise Him.   While
Christ had no sin *personally* to confess, He had sins *representatively*.   In one of the prophetic Psalms of His sufferings
He speaks of "My sins," "My reproach," and "My shame"
Ps. lxix. 5, 19).   Personally this could not be true of Him, but
representatively it was.   Rotherham's translation of Hebrews
i. 3 gives the same thought; it reads, "When He made
purification for Himself."   As the Head of the Church He
acted for His mystical body, in answering for the sin of the
members.   As God the Son, in the intrinsic worth of His
personality, there was no need for Him to make purification,
but as the Son of God, as the representative of the sons of

God, He acted for them, and thus in His action they acted. John's objection was overruled by Christ's word, "Suffer it to be so now, for thus it becometh us to fulfil all righteousness." Christ in figure met the claim of righteousness in dying for the sinner, that the believing sinner might have a claim to the righteousness which is by faith in Himself. The Holy Spirit has distinctly stated that Christ was numbered with the transgressors (Isa. liii. 12; Luke xxii. 37), and may we not say as a transgressor? Dr. Denney says, "It would not have been astonishing if Jesus had come from Galilee to baptise along with John, if He had taken His stand by John's side confronting the people; the astonishing thing is, being what He was, He came to be baptised and took His stand with the people. He identified Himself with them. As far as baptism could express it, He made all that was theirs His. . . . It was a great act of loving communion with our misery."

He was numbered with us in our misery, and we are now numbered with Him in His merit. It is not without significance that the word "numbered," which speaks of Christ being identified with sinners, is the same as applied to believers by God, when He reckons to them the worth of His Son.

The word translated *"reckon," "impute,"* and *"counted"* in Romans iv., which are one and the same in the Greek, is applied to Christ being reckoned with the thieves as a thief in Mark xv. 27; Luke xxii. 37.

Who baptised Christ? John. John was the representative of the majesty of God in law. He was the last of the prophets, who had to do with the Old Dispensation, hence, Christ says of him, in contrast to those who are in the Kingdom of Heaven, "He that is least in the Kingdom of

Heaven is greater than he" (Matt. xi. 11): not greater in character, but greater in privilege. Christ identifies Himself with John by saying of His baptism, "Thus it becometh *us* to fulfill all righteousness." Here are two parties, each has a role to perform. John's part is the part of God's Holy Law. The Law must inflict its penalty, or God's attributes are forfeited. Jesus' part is 'to put away sin by the sacrifice of Himself' (Heb. ix. 26), to be made sin for us (11. Cor. v. 21), to be made a curse (Gal. iii. 13), to once suffer for sins, the just for the unjust (1. Peter iii. 18). "So, it becometh us—thee and Me, each to bear His part."

Where did John baptise Jesus? In Jordan. Gosse says of the river Jordan, "The river, like so many things in Jehovah's land, was a symbol of solemn, mystic significance. Physically, it is a river absolutely unique in the whole world; cleft in the very bowels of the whole earth; being, at its issue from the Lake of Galilee, far below the sea level; and ever plunging lower and lower, by twenty-seven distinct descents, till it empties into the Dead Sea, that horrid, yawning chasm of salt and pitch, and desolation, whose surface is actually 1,300 feet below the Mediterranean; the awful grave of those guilty cities, which are 'set forth for an example, suffering the vengeance of eternal fire.' Throughout the Scripture this wondrous river of death stands as the type of penal death—of death issuing in hell. Its very name is a parable, whether we accept the etymology of the word, the 'downward plunger,' or the other which means 'the river of judgment'—the older and perhaps the better one."

Christ went beneath the waters of the downward plunger, this river of judgment. The whelming of waters is a frequent figure of the punitive wrath of God. One Hebrew word, which is frequently used, means to wash thoroughly, to drown, to overflow, and is frequently used to denote a calamity, an overflowing devastation (see Isa. viii. 8; x. 22; xxviii. 2, 15, 17; xxx. 28; xliii. 2).   It is used by Christ in Psalm lxix. 2, when He says, "I am come into deep waters where the floods *overflow Me*.". The same word as *"overflow"* is rendered *"drown"* in Song of Solomon viii. 7, where we read of love—"many waters cannot quench love, neither can the floods *drown* it."   Christ was drowned beneath the waters of judgment for us, but those waters could not drown His love for us, and now He assures us, because of what He has done for us, the waters "shall not *overflow* us" (Isa. xliii. 2).

2. *The Dying Corn of Wheat*

"Except a corn of wheat fall into the ground and die, it abideth alone; but if it die, it bringeth forth much fruit" (John xii. 24).   The association of the word *"except"* in John's Gospel lays down the rule—"A condition must be fulfilled before the end can be attained."

God's presence is a necessity to do His miracles—*"Except* God be with Him" (John iii. 2).

The new birth is a qualification to enter into and see the Kingdom of God—*"Except* a man be born again," etc. (John iii. 3).

The bestowment of a gift is a pre-requisite to its being received—*"Except* it be given" (John iii. 27).

The sinner must be drawn before he can come—*"Except* the Father draw him" (John vi. 44).

Eating is an essential to life—*"Except* ye eat the flesh of the Son of Man ye have no life in you" (John vi. 53).

Union is necessary to fruit-bearing—*"Except* ye abide in the Vine" (John xv. 4).

Death is necessary to life—"*Except* a corn of wheat," etc. (John xii. 24).

As long as the seed corn remains unburied it abides alone. When it is planted in the earth it seems to die, to be lost, but it begins to grow, and by-and-bye it brings forth fruit, fifty, sixty, or a hundredfold; even so with Christ. He would have been for ever alone had He not died for us, therefore, it was a necessity that He should go into the blackness of our death, that we might share the blessedness of His life. He went into the lostness of our desert, that we might have the livingness of His grace.

3. *The Uplifted Saviour*

Christ's solemn and emphatic affirmation about His death was—"The Son of Man *must* be lifted up" (John iii. 14). We hear Christ ringing the changes on the word *"must."* From His first recorded utterance till near His ascension He emphasizes the necessity of His mission. We have only to ponder His use of the word *"dei,"* and as we do so, we behold Christ under twelve different characters:

1. The Obedient Servant.—"I *must* be about My Father's business" (Luke ii. 49).

2. The Ardent Servant.—"I *must* work the works of Him that sent Me" (John ix. 4).

3. The Faithful Teacher.—"The Son of Man *must* suffer" (Mark viii. 31).

4. The Determined Walker.—"I *must* walk to-day," etc. (Luke xiii. 33).

5. The Expectant King.—"But first *must* He suffer" (Luke xvii. 25).

6. The Passover Lamb.—"The Passover *must* be killed" (Luke xxii. 7).

7. The Scripture Fulfiller.—"This that is written *must* be accomplished" (Luke xxii. 37).

8. The Crucified Christ.—"The Son of Man *must* be delivered into the hands of sinful men and be crucified" (Luke xxiv. 7).

9. The Explaining Lord.—*"Ought* not Christ to have suffered these things?" (Luke xxiv. 26).

10. The Unfolding Teacher.—"All things *must* needs be fulfilled" (Luke xxiv. 44).

11. The Gospel Personified.—"Thus it *behoved*" "Christ to suffer" (Luke xxiv. 46).

12. The Uplifted Saviour.—"The Son of Man *must* be lifted up" (John iii. 14).

Bengel says upon this word *"must"*—"For this purpose He came down from heaven." We must put it even stronger. He *had* to come if we were to be saved. His prayer in the Garden of Gethsemane lends color to this statement. He cried—"If it be possible, let this cup pass from Me"; and because it was an impossibility, He drained the cup to the dregs and went on to the bitter end till He could say, with satisfaction to heaven and earth, and the defeat of hell,—"It is finished."

CHRIST'S DEATH: ITS NATURE

There is no uncertain note in the teaching of Christ as to the nature of His atonement. He speaks of a momentous hour in His life's history (John xii. 27), a great gift He would bestow (John vi. 51), a substitutionary act He would perform (Matt. xxvi. 28), an exceptional work He would accomplish (Luke xii. 50), a unique love He would manifest (John xv. 9, 13), a vital blessing He would secure (John

xii. 24), and an unsurpassed glory He would, and did, render to His Father (John xvii. 4).

Christ's atonement was vocative in its calling. Christ again and again points to a crisis in His life's history by referring to a momentous hour into which He was to come. That hour was known and anticipated by Him, as may be gathered by the repeated sentence—"His hour was not yet come" (John vii. 30; viii. 20). When this hour's ominous shadow was creeping over Him, then we have the further statement, "The hour is come" (John xii. 23; xiii. 1; xvii. 1). The importance and intensity of that hour may be apprehended in Christ's interrogation to His Father about it when in heart's anguish He exclaimed, "Now is My soul troubled, and what shall I say? Father save me from this hour?" (margin). "But for this cause came I unto this hour" (John xii. 27). Christ felt He could not pray, "Father save Me from this hour," for that hour was the goal of His life. He was called to this hour of woe that we might know the hour of welcome, salvation, and life to which He refers in John v. 25. His star of destiny was the death of Calvary. He fulfilled the plan of the Father in going to the place of sacrifice.

Christ's atonement was vicarious in its act. Christ leaves us in no uncertainty about His death being vicarious. He says, "The Son of Man came . . . to give His life a ransom for many" (Matt. xx. 28). Without going into the usage of the preposition *"anti,"* rendered *"for,"* it is sufficient to remark its meaning is *"instead of."* "In His death everything was made His, that sin had made ours—everything in sin except its sinfulness." He put His death in all its value over against our sin in all its evil and condemnation.

Christ's atonement was voluntary in its gift. There was no compulsion laid upon Him, other than the impulsion of His own heart of love. Love compels by its impelling. There is no power which moves so mightily as love in the force of its intensity. The Holy Spirit loves to ring the bells of His voluntary love. The following Scripture sentences in which are the words "gave" and "give" illustrate the ministry of the Spirit in this direction:—

What did He give Himself for? "He *gave* Himself *for our sins*" (Gal. i. 4).

Why did He give Himself? "Who *loved* me and *gave* Himself for me?" (Gal. ii. 20).

What did He give in giving Himself? "Who *gave* Himself a *ransom* for all?" (1. Tim. ii. 6).

Who was it Who gave Himself? *"Christ* loved the Church and *gave* Himself for it" (Eph. v. 25).

What was the intent He had in giving Himself? "He *gave* Himself that He might *redeem us from all iniquity*" (Titus ii. 14).

The answers to the questions are found in the emphasized words in the Scripture sentence. Besides the above words of the Spirit embodying the voluntary act of Christ in His death, Christ Himself emphasized the same. He says, "The Son of Man came to *give* His life" (Matt. xx. 28). "The bread that I will *give* is My flesh" (John vi. 51); "The Good Shepherd *giveth* His life for the sheep" (John x. 11). His willingness to act for us brings out the intrinsic worth of His action.

Christ's atonement was valuable in its completion. The thought of failure never entered into the calculation of Christ. The conclusion to which He had come was the inclusion of all the Father had given Him to do, hence, His

dying triumphant cry was, "It is finished." That word
"finished" means to complete, to fulfill, to perfect. It is
rendered *"gone over"* in Matt. x. 23; *"pay"* in Matt. xvii.
24; *"performed"* in Luke ii. 39; *"accomplished"* in Luke xii.
50; xviii. 31; xxii. 37; John xix. 28; *"fulfil"* in James ii. 8;
"filled up" in Rev. xv. 1; *"expired"* in Rev. xx. 7; and *"finished"* in Rev. x. 7. If we embody these words in Christ's
work we begin to apprehend something of its greatness and
completeness. He has *"gone over"* all the will of God on
our behalf (Heb. x. 12); He has paid all the tribute asked
by God in His righteousness (1. Pet. i. 18, 19; Exo. xxx.
11-16); He has *"performed"* all the Father gave Him to do
(John xvii. 4); He has *"accomplished"* all the prophecies
predicted about Him (Luke xxiv. 44); He has *fulfilled"*
all the law of God in its double requirement of obedience
and death. His obedience shows His perfection, and in His
death He answers for the disobedient (Phil. ii. 8; Gal. iii.
13); He has *"filled up"* all the havoc made by sin in the
believer's life (Rom. v. 17-21); He has *"expired"* in death
on account of sin (11. Cor. v. 21); and He *"finished"* every
detail of the work which God set Him to perform (John
xix. 28-30).

What he undertook He consummated. In creation we
behold the perfection of His skilful hand, but in redemption
we see the production of His loving heart. "Whatsoever
the Lord doeth, it shall be for ever, nothing can be put to it,
nor anything taken from it, and God doeth it, that men
should fear before Him" (Eccles. iii. 14, R. V.).

Christ's atonement is vital in its application. Christ's last
act before He suffered was the institution of the Lord's
Supper. As He took the cup, He said, "This cup is the New
Testament in My blood, even that which is poured out for

you" (Luke xxii. 20, R. V.). The word *"ekchuno"* is rendered *"poured out"* in the Revised Version, and is stronger than *"shed"* as in the old version. *"Chuno"* comes from *"cheo,"* which means *to pour,* and *"ek"* means *out of,* hence, the compound word which signifies *to pour out.* *"Ekchuno"* is rendered *"spilled"* in speaking of the new wine bursting the old skins, into which it had been placed (Luke v. 37); *"gushed out"* in calling attention to what happened to Judas when he committed suicide, and his "bowels gushed out" (Acts i. 18); and it is given *"poured out"* in referring to the Holy Spirit being given to the Gentiles (Acts x. 45). Christ's life was spilled, poured out, shed on our behalf. There were no half measures, but an absolute dying out.

To *"pour out"* is a term which is frequently used in the Old Testament in connection with the offerings (Exo. xxix. 12; Lev. iv. 7, 18, 25, 30; viii. 15; xvii. 13). The blood poured out, and all of it, is typical of Christ Who poured out His soul unto death on our behalf. His life-giving is our life-bringing. The poured out life of His paschal offering has secured for us the Pentecostal blessing of the Spirit's abundant life. As the dead body of the man, which touched the dead body of Elisha, rose and revived and stood upon its feet (II. Kings xiii. 21); so contact with the Christ in His death brings life to us who were dead in sins. His death for sin saves us from the death of sin, and makes us dead to sin (I. Pet. ii. 24).

Christ's atonement is voiceful in its manifestation. As the Pleiades are said to be the hub of the universe, so Christ's word as to the love of God to the world is the centre of revelation. John iii. 16 is the Gospel in solution, grace in its essence, truth in its concrete, mercy in its ministry, love in its source, power in its attractibility, and the heart of

revelation. All God has to say and give are expressed by
the Living Word in the beauty of His peerless life, and the
provision of His sacrificial death. Verily, His death speak-
eth better things than that of Abel's for his blood cried for
swift and executed condemnation upon the murderer, but
Christ's blood proclaims just clearance from sin for the sinner. Christ is aptly called "The Word," for He tells out
in all He became, was, is, has done, is doing, and will do,
what God is.

> "Sorrow, sin and desolation,
>   These Thy claim to me.
> Love that won me full salvation,
>   This my claim to Thee."

Christ's atonement is voluminous in its glory. One of
the last statements of Christ to His Father was, "I have
glorified Thee on the earth and finished the work Thou
gavest Me to do" (John xvii. 4). Man had not only sinned,
but he had come short of the glory of God. Christ answered
for both, for He was not only the Sin-offering bearing the
judgment due to sin, but He was the Burnt-offering, bringing glory to God by the sweet savour of His perfect obedience unto death. The glory of God's handiwork is seen in
creation, but the splendor of His heart-work is unveiled at
the cross. The glory of God's grace, the glory of His truth,
the glory of His love, the glory of His wisdom, the glory of
His riches, the glory of His compassion, and the glory of
His worth, are all unfolded and enhanced in the glory which
Christ made known, "the glory of the Only-Begotten, full
of grace and truth."

8
The Holy Spirit
and Christ's Atonement

There is one book in the Bible where the Holy Spirit is not mentioned by name, and that book is Leviticus. He is like the auctioneer that Dr. A. A. Bonar used to speak about, who was describing the beauty of an oil painting while he was hidden behind it. The Spirit is the unseen author in the book of Leviticus, like the life in the blood which makes it a life-giving fluid (Lev. xvii. 11, R. V.), for while He is unseen He is none the less there, as He unfolds to us the essential and blessed truth of atonement.

There are two things to which attention is called in thinking of the Holy Spirit's testimony in reference to Christ's atoning sacrifice, and these are the Greek prepositions used in connection with it, and the qualifying expressions which are applied to Christ's blood.

1. *The Prepositions and the Atonement.*

There are seven prepositions found in association with Christ's death for sin, and these are "Peri," (περὶ), "Huper," (ὑπέρ), "Anti," (ἀντί), "Dia," (διά), "Eis," (εἰς), "En," (ἐν), "Sun," (σύν); and these are classified under the following words, Proclamation, Provision, Substitution, Mediation, Intention, Permanence and Identification.

PROCLAMATION

Peri. (περὶ) With the genitive, *"Peri"* signifies action around an object, hence, to speak or hear *about,* or *of* a thing or person. It is used in connection with Christ when He referred to the Holy Spirit as, "this spake He *of* (*Peri*) the Spirit (John vii. 39), and is translated *concerning* (*peri*) when reference is made to the people murmuring about Christ (John vii. 12, 32). This preposition is used in connection with Christ and His atonement in the following passages.

The Covenant-Obtainer.—"My blood which is shed *for* (*peri*) many" (Matt. xxvi. 28; Mark xiv. 24).

The Cleansing-Giver.—"Go shew thyself to the priest, and offer *for* (*peri*) thy cleansing" (Luke v. 14).

The Scripture-Fulfiller.—"He expounded unto them in all the Scriptures the things *concerning* (*peri*) Himself" (Luke xxiv. 27). "All things must be fulfilled, which were written in the law of Moses, and in the prophets, and in the psalms *concerning* (*peri*) Me" (Luke xxiv. 44).

The Condemned Sufferer.—" God sending His Own Son in the likeness of sinful flesh, and *for* (*peri*) sin, condemned sin in the flesh" (Rom. viii. 3).

The Satisfying-Atoner.—"As *for* (*peri*) the people, so also *for* (*peri*) Himself, to offer *for* (*huper*) sins" (Heb. v. 3).

The Willing Victim.—"In burnt offerings and sacrifices *for* (*peri*) sin, Thou hast had no pleasure" (Heb. x. 6).

The Sufficient Saviour.—"Now where remission of these is, there is no more offering *for* (*peri*) sin" (Heb. x. 18).

The Sin-Consumer.—"For the bodies of those beasts, whose blood is brought into the sanctuary by the high priest *for* (*peri*) sin, are burned without the camp" (Heb. xiii. 11).

The Blessing-Bringer.—"Christ also hath once suffered *for* (*peri*) sins, the Just for the unjust, that He might bring us to God" (1. Peter iii. 18).

The Propitiation-Obtainer.—"He is the propitiation *for* (*peri*) our sins" (1. John ii. 2; iv. 10).

There are two thoughts throbbing through these Scriptures, namely: Christ's action concerning sin in dying for it, and the Spirit's testimony concerning Him in His death, either directly or by typical reference.

PROVISION

Huper. (ὑπέρ) With the genitive, *huper* means one object bending over another for its protection, hence, to favor, care, benefit, and act for the sake of another. A mother bird bending over her young, in protecting them from danger, illustrates the meaning of the word. The Spirit uses the preposition in speaking of the Spirit's "intercession *for* (*huper*) us" (Rom. viii. 26), of Christ's "intercession *for* (*huper*) us" (Rom. viii. 34), of God being *"for* (*huper*) us" (Rom. viii. 31), and of believers having a "care one *for* (*huper*) another" (1. Cor. xii. 25). As applied to Christ's death the main thought is, the provision which is made on behalf of fallen humanity, in His atoning sacrifice, so that men may be saved from the consequence of sin. Huper occurs over thirty times in this provisional sense, and underneath there is the underlying thought of substitution, hence, the word is rendered in Philemon 13 *"in stead"* where Paul speaks to Philemon of Onesimus and says, "Whom I would have retained with me, that *in* thy stead (*huper*) he might have ministered unto me in the bonds of the gospel."

The Gracious Giver.—"This is My body which is given *for* (*huper*) you" (Luke xxii. 19).

The Sufficient Atoner.—"My blood which is shed *for* (*huper*) you" Luke xxii. 20).

The Divine Supplier.—"My flesh, which I will give *for* (*huper*) the life of the world" (John vi. 51).

The Good Shepherd.—"The Good Shepherd giveth His life *for* (*huper*) the sheep" (John x. 11).

The Faithful Actor.—"I lay down My life *for* (*huper*) the sheep" (John x. 15).

The Proclaimed Substitute.—"One man should die *for* (*huper*) the people" (John xi. 50).

The Specified Saviour.—"Jesus should die *for* (*huper*) that nation" (John xi. 51).

The Universal Provider.—"Not *for* (*huper*) that nation only" (John xi. 52).

The Consecrated Lord.—"*For* (*huper*) their sakes I sanctify Myself" (John xvii. 19).

The Announced Intervener.—"Expedient that one man should die *for* (*huper*) the people" (John xviii. 14).

The Strong Deliverer.—"Christ died *for* (*huper*) the ungodly" (Rom. v. 6).

The Dying Christ.—"Christ died *for* (*huper*) us" (Rom. v. 8).

The Delivered Son.—"Delivered Him up *for* (*huper*) us all" (Rom. viii. 32).

The Sacrificed Passover.—"Christ our passover is sacrificed *for* (*huper*) us" (1. Cor. v. 7).

The Remembered Sufferer.—"My body which is broken *for* (*huper*) you" (1. Cor. xi. 24).

The Sin-Bearer.—"Christ died *for* (*huper*) our sins" (1. Cor. xv. 3).

The Holy Kinsman.—"One died *for* (*huper*) all, therefore all died" (11. Cor. v. 14, R. V.).

The Glorious Purposer.—"He died *for* (*huper*) all, that they which live should not henceforth live unto themselves (11. Cor. v. 15).

The Emphatic Emphasizer.—"But unto Him Who died *for* (*huper*) them, and rose again" (11. Cor. v. 15).

The Sin Offering.—"Made Him to be sin *for* (*huper*) us" (II. Cor. v. 21).

The Trespass Offering.—"Who gave Himself *for* (*huper*) our sins" (Gal. i. 4).

The Surrendered Lover.—"Gave Himself *for* (*huper*) me" (Gal. ii. 20).

The Curse Receiver.—"Made a curse *for* (*huper*) us" (Gal. iii. 13).

The Burnt Offering.—"Given Himself *for* (*huper*) us" (Eph. v. 2).

The Church Sanctifier.—"Loved the Church, and gave Himself *for* (*huper*) it" (Eph. v. 25).

The Glory Obtainer.—"Who died *for* (*huper*) us" (I. Thes. v. 10).

The Unique Ransomer.—"Who gave Himself a ransom *for* (*huper*) all" (I. Tim. ii. 6).

The Practical Redeemer.—"Who gave Himself *for* (*huper*) us" (Titus ii. 14).

The Death Taster.—"Taste death *for* (*huper*) every man" (Heb. ii. 9).

The Typical Priest.—"Ordained *for* (*huper*) men." "Offer . . . sacrifices *for* (*huper*) sins." "To offer *for* (*huper*) sins" (Heb. v. 1, 3).

The Perfect Offerer.—"Offered one sacrifice *for* (*huper*) sins" (Heb. x. 12).

The Perfect Example.—"Christ also suffered *for* (*huper*) us" (I. Peter ii. 21).

The Introducer to God.—"Suffered *for* (*huper*) sins, the Just *for* (*huper*) the unjust to bring us to God" (I. Peter iii. 18).

The Sin Conquerer.—"As Christ hath suffered *for* (*huper*) us in the flesh" (I. Peter iv. 1).

The Love Inspirer.—"Because He laid down His life *for* (*huper*) us, and we ought to lay down our lives *for* (*huper*) the brethren" (1. John iii. 16).

SUBSTITUTION

"Anti." (αντι) *"Anti"* signifies one thing over against another, one thing in the place of another, or something given in exchange for something else. In a popular sense the word *"instead"* illustrates its meaning. It is used in the following senses. One reigning in the stead of another—"Archelaus reigned *in the room* (*anti*) of his father Herod" (Matt. ii. 22); an equivalent given for a loss—"An eye *for* (*anti*) an eye, and a tooth *for* (*anti*) a tooth" (Matt. v. 38); the payment of a claim—"Give unto them *for* (*anti*) Me and thee" (Matt. xvii. 27); something given in the place of something else—"Will he *for* (*anti*) a fish give him a serpent?" (Luke xi. 11); a given thing taking the place of another—"Grace *for* (*anti*) grace" (John i. 16); something which is not to be given in the place of what is given—"Recompense to no man evil *for* (*anti*) evil" (Rom. xii. 17; 1. Thes. v. 15; 1. Pet. iii. 9); a woman's long hair is in the place of a covering, "her hair is given *for* (*anti*) a covering" (1. Cor. xi. 15); when a man takes a wife and leaves his parents—"*for* (*anti*) this cause shall a man leave his father and mother, and shall be joined unto his wife" (Eph. v. 31); when one sets aside one thing for another, hence, Christ *"for* (*anti*) the joy that was set before Him endured the cross"* (Heb. xii. 2); the same thought is expressed when Esau sold his birthright *"for* (*anti*) one morsel of meat"* (Heb. xii. 16); and when the believer is exhorted to put the will of God in the place of his own *"for* (*anti*) ye ought to say if the Lord will"* (Jas. iv. 15).

"Anti" is used by Christ when He said the purpose of His
death was, to "give His life a ransom *for (anti)* many"
(Matt. xx. 28; Mark x. 45). *"Anti"* is found in combination with *"Lutron"* (which means loosing money) and is
rendered *"Ransom"* in 1. Tim. ii. 6. *"Antilutron"* therefore means a ransom paid instead of others having to pay it.
Man was the slave of Satan, sold under sin. He was unable
to ransom himself, because absolute obedience is due to
God, therefore no act of ours can satisfy for the least
offence. Leviticus xxv. 48, allowed one sold captive to be
redeemed by one of his brethren. The Son of God therefore became man that He might redeem us, *"Anti-lutron"*
implies not merely ransom, but a substituted or an equivalent
ransom, the *"anti"* implying vicarious substitution.

MEDIATION

Dia (δια). With the genitive *"Dia"* signifies, by means
of, a procuring cause which brings something to someone
else. It is of frequent occurrence in connection with Christ
and His death. We shall note some of the blessings which
flow from His death, as illustrating the meaning of the
preposition.

Salvation.—*"Through (dia)* Him might be saved"* (John
iii. 17; x. 9).

Life.—"Live *by (dia)* Me" (John vi. 57).

Purchased.—"Church of God which He **hath purchased**
with (dia) His own blood" (Acts xx. 28).

Approach.—"No man cometh unto the Father but *by
(dia)* Me" (John xiv. 6).

Redemption.—"In whom we have redemption *through
(dia)* His blood" (Eph. i. 7).

Reconciliation.—"Reconciled to God *by* (*dia*) the death of His Son" (Rom. v. 10).

Righteousness.—"So *by* (*dia*) the obedience of one shall many be made righteous" (Rom. v. 19).

Victory.—"I thank God *through* (*dia*) Jesus Christ our Lord" (Rom. vii. 25; viii. 37; 1. Cor. xv. 57).

Resurrection.—"*By* (*dia*) Man came also the resurrection of the dead" (1. Cor. xv. 21).

Adoption.—"Predestinated us unto the adoption of children *by* (*dia*) Jesus Christ" (Eph. i. 5).

Access.—"*Through* (*dia*) Him we both have access by one Spirit unto the Father" (Eph. ii. 18).

Peace.—"Made peace *through* (*dia*) the blood of His cross" (Col. i. 20).

Atonement.—"*By* (*dia*) Himself purged our sins" (Heb. i. 3).

Deliverance.—"*Through* (*dia*) death He might destroy him that hath the power of death" (Heb. ii. 14).

Sanctification.—"*Through* (*dia*) the offering of the body of Jesus Christ" (Heb. x. 10); "Sanctify the people *with* (*dia*) His own blood" (Heb. xiii. 12).

INTENTION

"*Eis*" (εἰς) is a preposition governing the accusative, with the primary idea of motion *into* any place or thing. Heb. ix. 24, gives a good illustration of its meaning—"Christ is not entered *into* (*eis*) the holy place made with hands . . . but *into* (*eis*) heaven itself, now to appear in the presence of God for us." A person approaching *unto* a place in order to enter *into* it expresses the full meaning of *eis*. As applied to Christ's death there are two thoughts, namely: Christ approaching the place of His death and entering into all its suffering, and the benefit into which He now brings us in consequence.

The purpose of Christ's death.—"He appeared *to* (*eis*) put away sin by the sacrifice of Himself" (Heb. ix. 26).

The meaning of Christ's death.—"Christ was once offered *to* (*eis*) bear the sins of many" (Heb. ix. 28).

The reconciliation by Christ's death.—"To reconcile all things *unto* (*eis*) Himself" (Col. i. 20).

The identity with Christ's death.—"With Him by baptism *into* (*eis*) death" (Rom. vi. 3, 4).

The moulding of Christ's death.—"That form of doctrine whereto (Literally, '*unto*,' '*eis*') ye were delivered" (Rom. vi. 17, margin).

The claim of Christ's death.—"We are the Lord's: for *to* this *end* (*eis*) Christ both died and lived again, that He might be Lord, etc. (Rom. xiv. 9).

The remembrance of Christ's death.—"This do *in* (*Eis*, Lit. unto) remembrance of Me" (1. Cor. xi. 24).

PERMANENCE

"*En*" (ἐν) occurs between two and three thousand times in the New Testament. The preposition, governing the dative, signifies one object resting in another, hence believers are said to be "*in* (*en*) Christ" as resting in Him (Eph. i. 4) for life (11. Tim. i. 1), redemption (Eph. i. 7), acceptance (Eph. i. 6), nearness (Eph. ii. 13), liberty (Rom. viii. 2), union (2. Cor. xii. 5), and sanctification (1. Cor. i. 2).

As found in association with Christ's blood, "*en*" speaks of the permanence of the blessings which are found therein and secured thereby.

Justification in Christ's blood.—"Much more then being justified *by (en)* His blood" (Rom. v. 9).

Nearness in Christ's blood.—"Now *in (en)* Christ Jesus ye . . . are made nigh *by (en)* the blood of Christ" (Eph. ii. 13).

Entrance in Christ's blood.—"Having therefore, brethren, boldness to enter into the holiest *by (en)* the blood of Jesus" (Heb. x. 19).

Perfection in Christ's blood.—"*Through (en)* the blood of the everlasting covenant" (Heb. xiii. 20).

Redemption in Christ's blood.—"Thou wast slain, and hast redeemed us to God *by (en)* Thy blood" (Rev. v. 9).

Beauty in Christ's blood.—"Made them white *in (en)* the blood of the Lamb" (Rev. vii. 14).

Consecrated in Christ's blood.—"This cup is the New Testament *in (en)* My blood" (1. Cor. xi. 25).

IDENTIFICATION

Sun (σὺν) governing only the dative and speaks of intimate association, co-operation, oneness, and union. It is generally rendered *"with,"* hence, believers are said to be "quickened *with* Christ" (Col. ii. 13), our "life is hid *with* Christ in God" (Col. iii. 3), and when He comes back for us, we shall "live together *with* Him" (1. Thes. v. 10), "appear *with* Him in glory" (Col. iii. 4), and shall be "for ever *with* the Lord" (1. Thes. iv. 17). Believers are also said to be "dead *with (sun)* Christ" in His death (Rom. vi. 8; Col. ii. 20), even as the two thieves were "crucified *with (sun)* Him" (Matt. xxvii. 38).

"Sun" is also found in combination with another word, *"Sustauroo,"* which means to be impaled on a cross in company with others; hence is rendered *"crucified with"* in

referring to the thieves who were crucified with Christ (Matt. xxvii. 44; Mark xv. 27; John xix. 32), and also in speaking of the old man of the sinful habits it is said to be "Crucified *with*" Christ (Rom. vi. 6) and the "I" of the self life, as Paul says, "I am *crucified with Christ*" (Gal. ii. 20).

II. *The qualifying expressions which are applied to the blood of Christ*

The one expression which is prominent in the New Testament about the blood of Christ is, "without shedding of blood is no remission" (Heb. ix. 22). This is the inspired statement of the Spirit. By sin we had forfeited everything. By the giving of the life of the Son of God He more than regains what we had lost. The shedding of blood always presupposes the giving up of the life of Christ on our behalf. Jehovah said long ago, "For the life of the flesh is in the blood: and I have given it to you upon the altar to make atonement for your souls: for it is the blood that maketh atonement by reason of the life (Lev. xvii. 11, R. V.).

There are a number of different expressions associated with Christ's blood.

"The blood of the New Covenant" (Luke xxii. 20, R. V.; Heb. x. 29), speaks of the abrogation of the old covenant in all its sacrifices, and the institution of the new covenant with all its blessings. Christ has signed and sealed the covenant with His own precious blood.

"The blood of Jesus" proclaims the perfection of the human life of the Man of men, who gave Himself for the sons of men and has thus obtained for us the right of entrance where He is (Heb. x. 19).

The blood of God (Acts xx. 28). The Church of God is said to have been purchased with His own blood, therefore the coin which has acquired the assembly of the redeemed is Divine.

"The blood of Jesus Christ" (1. Pet. i. 2). When the names of Jesus Christ come in the order, "Jesus Christ," the starting point is from the Jesus who lived and died to the Christ who is seated and glorified. The cradle of His incarnation must culminate in the throne of His acceptance *via* the cross of His expiation.

The blood of Christ Jesus. "Christ Jesus, whom God hath set forth to be a propitiation through faith in His blood" (Rom. iii. 24, 25). When the names Christ Jesus follow in the order, "Christ Jesus," the starting point is from the seat of His acceptance at the right hand of His Father to the manger of His humiliation, *via* the Calvary of His atonement. Where He is, what He did, and what He became are the sheet anchors which hold us to the eternal Rock of Ages.

"The blood of Jesus Christ His Son" (1. John i. 7). The emphasis in this sentence is on "His Son." The worth of His work in its permanent value must be computed by the worth of Himself. The place which the Son has obtained by His propitiation on the cross is the place of fellowship which He retains for the sons on the same ground.

"The blood of Christ" (Heb. ix. 14). "Christ" speaks of the anointed of God. He was qualified by the Holy Spirit to answer for our sins, and now He is the Anointer to give us the Holy Spirit that our sins may never master us.

"The blood of the Lord" (1. Cor. xi. 27). The title of Christ as Lord reminds us of His proprietary right over us, and our responsibility to Him is to recognize whose we are and whom we serve, hence, to remember His death in an unworthy manner proclaims our want of loyalty to Him.

The blood of the Beloved. "Accepted in the Beloved"

(Eph. i. 6, 7). Christ as the Beloved is the special object of God's affection, therefore to be blessed through His blood means that we, too, are honoured subjects of His grace.

"The precious blood of Christ" (1. Pet. i. 19). Rarity, speciality, worth and value are suggested by the word "precious," and especially the last, for His blood is invaluable and beyond all estimation.

"The blood of His cross" (Col. i. 20). The cross in Scripture is always associated with suffering. He died the worst kind of death for the worst kind of people, and now He can make them the best kind of saints and lift them up to the highest place in glory.

"The blood of sprinkling" (Heb. xii. 24). As there was a difference in the blood poured out and the blood sprinkled, in the Levitical economy, so there is a difference between the death of Christ for us and the application of that death to us. The former speaks of salvation provided, and the latter of salvation received.*

---

*The difference between salvation provided in the death of Christ, and the acceptance of the provision made is very well illustrated in the following incident. In 1829 or 1830, George Wilson, in Pennsylvania, was sentenced to be hanged, by a United States Court in Philadelphia, for robbing the mails and murder. Andrew Jackson, as President of the United States, pardoned him, but Wilson refused the pardon and insisted that it was not a pardon unless he accepted it. That was a point in law never before raised in the U. S. of A. The Attorney General said the law was silent on the point. The President was urged to call upon the Supreme Court to decide the point at once, as the Sheriff must know whether to hang Wilson or not. Chief Justice John Marshall, one of the ablest lawyers, gave the following decision: "A pardon is a paper, the value of which depends upon its acceptance by the person implicated. It is hardly to be supposed that one under sentence of death, would refuse to accept a pardon, but if it is refused, it is no pardon. George Wilson must be hanged." And he was hanged. Who is responsible for his death? No one but the man himself. The law said he must die. The President stepped in between him and the law, but the man refused the pardon.

Indirectly, the Supreme Court of the U. S., decided that the truth of the atonement of Christ, in making provision for the salvation of the whole world, is only beneficial to those who receive Him as their own personal Saviour. The righteousness of God is *unto* all in its *offer*, but it is *upon* them that believe in its *benefit* (Rom. iii. 22).

The blood of the everlasting covenant (Heb. xiii. 20).
The emphasis here is on the adjective, *"aionios,"* for the
blessings which the blood of Christ secures are eternal.

"The blood of the Lamb" (Rev. vii. 14; xii. 11). The
book of the Revelation is the only book which speaks of
"the blood of the Lamb," and it is not without meaning that
it should be thus spoken of in the book of the last things,
for the kingly Christ of the coming glory is seen in all the
fresh value of His atoning sacrifice, hence, He is represented
as a little Lamb newly slain.

Christ frequently emphasized the necessity of the shedding of His life's blood and the consequent outcome of
blessing in the words "My blood" (Matt. xxvi. 28; Mark
xiv. 24; Luke xxii. 20; John vi. 54, 55, 56; 1. Cor. xi. 25);
and the Holy Spirit frequently draws attention to the ben-
efits of Christ's atonement by using the words "His own
blood" and "His blood" (Acts xx. 28; Rom. iii. 25; v. 9;
Eph. i. 7; Col. i. 14; Heb. ix. 12; xiii. 12; Rev. i. 5; v. 9).

9

Satan and Christ's Atonement

The atonement of Christ affects heaven, earth, and hell. Heaven is satisfied with the atonement of Christ. Ample provision is made for earth's sin in it, and hell is defeated by it.

There is one expression, which is frequently used in the Epistle to the Hebrews, and that is, "The blood of bulls and goats." Whenever this expression is used, the reference is to the offering on the great day of atonement. The blood of the bullock was offered to Jehovah in making an atonement for Aaron and his house, and the two goats are associated in making an atonement for the sins of the people. Only one of the goats was killed, and the other goat was to be for Azazel, as the Revised Version states in Leviticus xvi. 10, for the scapegoat. Many theories have been advanced as to what is meant by Azazel, the consensus of opinion being that it has a reference to Satan. Some of the fathers even went so far as to say that Christ in His death met a certain claim of the evil one. But he, being a usurper, there was no claim to be met; still, since he had gained power over man through sin, that power had to be annulled, and this could only be done by Christ's sacrificial death.

I. *The Head bruised*

The prophetic statement given by Jehovah to Adam in the garden was that the seed of the woman should bruise the serpent's head (Genesis iii. 15). The pronoun "it" should be "he." It is masculine and not neuter. A better

reading, therefore, would be, "He shall bruise his head."
Many have thought that a reference is made to this declaration in Psalm xl. 7: certainly Heb. x, 7 lends colour to it,
for it may be rendered, "In the first roll, at the head of the
beginning of the book, it is written of Me, to do Thy will,
O My God."

The completeness of Christ's victory over the evil one is
indicated in the word "bruise." Parkhurst, in his Hebrew
lexicon, says upon this verb, "It means 'to cover,' 'overwhelm,' as with a tempest or darkness." Job ix. 17—"Who
will *overwhelm* me with a tempest." Psalm cxxxix. 11—
"Surely the darkness will *cover* me." This latter text, compared with the context, appears to me to fix the meaning of
the verb, and, therefore, according to the common reading,
I am obliged to understand it in the same sense in the
only remaining passage where it occurs, namely, Genesis
iii. 15, which, in this view, will contain an allusion to that
outer darkness to which Satan should finally be condemned,
as well as to that darkness of death and the grave to which
the mortal part of the promised Seed should be reduced,
when the power of darkness prevailed against Him (Luke
xxii. 53).

Satan seemed to overwhelm Christ when he focussed all
the powers of darkness upon Him at the cross. But he
was only bruising the heel of Christ. Christ by means of
that very death has overwhelmed the power of darkness,
and covered it with eternal confusion. Satan has bruised
the heel of Christ, but Christ has fetched him such a blow
on the head that he will never get over it.

II. *The Spoiler spoiled*

"He shall divide the spoil with the strong," or, as
Lowth renders it, "He shall take the spoil from the strong."

And we are given the reason wny He shall accomplish this, "because He hath poured out His soul unto death" (Isaiah liii. 12). Satan was the strong man armed that kept his goods in peace till Christ the Stronger overcame him, taking his armour from him. and dividing his spoils (Luke xi. 21, 22).

The Old Testament opens with the temptation of the first Adam, and the New Testament opens with the temptation of the last Adam. But what a contrast! In the former we behold defeat and ruin, but in the latter victory and redemption. In both temptations we see that Satan uses three weapons: the lust of the flesh, the lust of the eyes, and the pride of life.

Lust of the flesh—

"Tree was good for food" (Genesis iii. 6).

"Command that these stones be made bread" (Matt. iv. 3).

Lust of the eyes—

"Pleasant to the eyes" (Genesis iii. 6).

"Showed Him all the kingdoms" (Luke iv. 5).

Pride of life—

"Desired to make one wise" (Genesis iii. 6).

"Cast Thyself down" (Matt. iv. 6).

Eve met the temptations with her own words, but Christ met Satan's suggestions with the Word of God. Our first parents were alone in the garden of Eden when beguiled by the evil one, but our Saviour, ere He went into the wilderness, had passed through the waters of death, and had received the anointing of the Spirit's power. The secret of His victory in the wilderness is found in that He had first died in the waters of Jordan.

III. *The Powers stripped*

"Having spoiled principalities and powers He made a
show of them openly, triumphing over them in it," (Colossians ii. 15), that is, the Cross. The thought that is suggested is that Christ's victory over the powers of evil was
by means of the cross. The Revised Version reads, "Having put off from Himself the principalities and powers, He
made a show of them openly, triumphing over them in it."
Here the thought seems to be that of the powers and forces
of evil gathering around Christ, but He puts them off from
Himself, as a man would put off a garment which impedes
his action. Rotherham's rendering is "having stripped the
principalities and authorities," &c. I am inclined to think
that this last rendering is the more correct. The word
"spoiled" is used in Col. iii. 9, and is there rendered "have
put off"; while a cognate noun is found in ii. 11, and is
translated "the putting off." It means either having put
off from oneself, or having stripped others for oneself.
Liddle and Scott say that the expression is used in relation
to one who puts off his clothes for combat. Christ stripped
the principalities, as one might be stripped of his clothes.
Dr Maclaren remarks, "We see the whole process before
our eyes—the victor stripping his prisoners of their clothes,
of arms and ornaments and dress, then parading them as
his captives, and then dragging them at the wheels of his
triumphal car." The powers of hell are degraded and
humiliated by the death of Christ. They thought they
degraded and humiliated Him when they fixed Him to
Calvary's cross, but He transfixed and degraded them in
that very degradation. He stooped to conquer, and He conquered by means of His stoop.

IV. *Death's Authority overthrown*

"Forasmuch then as the children are partakers of flesh and blood, He also Himself likewise took part of the same; that through death He might destroy him that had the power of death, that is, the devil" (Hebrews ii. 14). There are two thoughts among others which are suggested by these words. First, the power Satan had. He is described as having the power of death. Satan evidently had great dominion and strength before Christ's death. The Greek word *"kratos"* suggests this. It is rendered dominion in I. Peter iv. 11; v. 11; Jude 25; and Rev. i. 6 in ascribing dominion to God. It is rendered *"strength"* in Luke i. 51, and *"power"* in Ephesians i. 19 and vi. 10, in speaking of the power of God's might. This very word being associated with Satan, at once suggests the greatness of his domain and might. The second thought is that Christ has taken away this power by means of His death. The word *"destroyed"* is translated *"loosed"* (Romans vii. 2), *"done away"* (1 Cor. xiii. 10), *"put down"* (1 Cor. xv. 24), *"ceased"* (Gal. v. 11), and *"abolished"* (11 Tim. i. 10). Each of these words might be read instead of "destroyed," and may be employed by way of illustration in showing how completely Christ has conquered. Christ has loosed the spirits of the Old Testament saints from the dominion of Satan. He has done away with the crippling power of hell. He has put away the greatness of the authority he once exercised. He has put down the authority of evil. He has made to cease that which prevailed before He died, and abolished the power of death by means of His own death, so that Christ stands before us and says, "I am . . . the Living One; and I was dead, and behold, I am alive for evermore, and I have the keys of death and of Hades (Revelation i. 18, R. V.).

"A fisherman, when he casts his angle into the river, doth not throw his hook in bare, naked, and uncovered, for then he knows the fish will never bite, and, therefore, he hides the hook within a worm, or some other bait, and so, the fish, biting at the worm, is caught by the hook. Thus Christ, coming to perform the great work of our redemption, did cover and hide His Godhead within the worm of His human nature. The grand water serpent, Leviathan, the devil, thinking to swallow the worm of His humanity, was caught by the hook of His Divinity. The hook stuck in his jaws, and tore him very sore. By thinking to destroy Christ, he destroyed his own kingdom, and lost his own power forever."

What does Christ's victory mean to us? We have to do with a conquered foe. Christ's conquest is a pledge of our victory. Let us by faith remember that He has delivered us from the power of darkness that we might walk in the light (Colossians i. 13); He was manifested to destroy the works of the devil, therefore, let us allow the Spirit of God to fully accomplish that purpose in us (1. John iii. 8); God's command is, Resist the devil, and he will flee from you, and flee he will if we resist him with the truth (1 Peter v. 9). He charges us to have on the whole armour that we may stand against the contending forces of evil (Ephesians vi. 10-18). He assures us that Satan shall be bruised under our feet (Romans xvi. 20); and as we keep in the power of His death, we shall have victory, like those we read of in the Word, who overcame him because of the blood of the Lamb, and because of the word of their testimony (Rev. xii. 11).

10
Holiness and Christ's Atonement

The atonement of Christ was not only an expiation for sin, but a triumph over it. Christ answered for sin that we should cease to answer to it. His death for sin is the death of sin. His passion for us quenches the passion of sin. The outward crucifixion of Christ which procures the benefit of pardon is the inward power which gives us to experience the inward crucifixion of self.

Sir Noel Paton's picture, *Death the Gate of Life,* has a meaning other than in the mind of the artist. A weary knight, wounded in his conflict with evil, has passed through the valley of the shadow of death, and is represented as kneeling in deep humility at the entrance of light and life. He has put off his helmet with the crest of falcon wings and peacock feathers—emblems of worldly ambition and pride. The belt and sword which are cast aside, and the armour which is falling off, indicate the renunciation of his own strength. The overblown hemlock, rank weeds, and withered branches on this side of the veil speak of sin's deadly poison, and of disappointed hopes, while the white lilies and wild roses on the other side tell of the purity and joy which blossom there. The permanence of the life he is entering is indicated by a clear and steadfast star which shines in the sky, while the waning moon on the horizon typifies the mutability of the life he is leaving behind.

The death of Christ is the gate of the spiritual life. No one lives to purpose who does not know the purport of that death. The lowliness of the cross is the death of pride and the life of humility; the separation of the cross means the severance from sin, and sanctification to the Lord; the manifestation of the cross is the unfolding of love and the inspiration of all love; the passion of the cross quenches the passion of evil desire, and impassionates with a holy fire of devotion; the blood of the cross cleanses from the pollution of sin and the pleasures of iniquity; the world's act of murder in crucifying Christ, removes the believer from the company of the world's fellowship; and the death of the cross is the death to everything not in the will of God.

There are certain words, Calvary words, which have a new meaning begotten within them because of their association with the Christ of Calvary—

CRUCIFIXION

There are four things which are said to be crucified in the crucifixion of Christ, namely, the old man, self, the flesh, and the world.

The Old Man. "Knowing this our old man is crucified with Him" (Romans vi. 6). The compound word rendered *"crucified with"* means co-crucifixion. To crucify means to impale on a stake, and co-crucifixion means to be crucified in company with others, as when the thieves were crucified with Christ. "The old man," which was crucified with Christ, is the sum total of the old self life, as made up by sin. The man of old is the old man in the totality of sin. When the Gibeonites came to Joshua, they came with "old sacks, old wine skins, old clothes, and old clouted shoes, and dry and mouldy bread." Professedly the old things with the old past of their lives. The whole lot of old rubbish should have been burnt, and they themseves killed, but they caught Joshua napping, and got past him by their craft. Our Joshua was not caught napping: the whole of our old habits formed in sin were condemned on the cross, and died there the death they deserved, and they are therefore no longer dominating us, for His death ended their existence.

Self Crucified. "I am crucified with Christ" (Galatians ii. 20). Here, again, it is co-crucifixion. If a dead leaf-stalk is examined it will be found that the old channel is silted by a barrier invisible to the naked eye. On last year's leaf the plant has shut the door, condemning it to decay, and soon, without further effort, the stalk loosens, the winds play around it, and it falls away. The cross of Christ shuts off the life of self, and is a barrier which stands between us and it, as we reckon we have died with Him. The title of a sermon read *"Self crucifixion the secret of a spiritual life."* No, that is the blunder which many are making, it is not self crucifixion, but crucifixion with Christ. It is not putting ourselves to death, but believing we are put to death in the death of Christ. The one is useless trying, and the other is unfailing triumph.

The Flesh Crucified. "They that are Christ's have crucified the flesh with the affections and lusts thereof" (Gal. v. 24). The flesh denotes the principle of life in man which is alienated from God, incurably and unmendably bad. As the blood of Christ brings us nigh to God, so this death kills that which caused us to go away from Him. The way to overcome the flesh and its works is to die with Christ to the flesh which works.

The World Crucified. "The world is crucified unto Me, and I unto the world" (Galatians vi. 14). The world, generally speaking is—

"Whatever passes as a cloud between,
The mental eye of faith and things unseen,
Causing that brighter world to disappear,
Or seem less lovely or its hope less dear,
That is our world, our idol, though it bear
Affections impress, or devotions air."

To the world, and all that is in it, we are crucified. We read of the debarring wisdom of the world (1. Corinthians i, 21), the evil character of the world (Galatians i. 4), the course of the world (Ephesians ii. 2), the dominating darkness of the world (Ephesians vi. 12), the opposition of the friendship of the world (James iv. 4), the deadening power of the corruption in the world (11. Peter i. 4), the contamination of the pollutions of the world (11. Peter ii. 20), and the trinity of the things of the world (1. John ii. 15). To all of these we are crucified, and they are to be to us as dead things, and then we shall be as a dead thing to the world. If we see the world on the cross, the world will see us on the cross.

Professor Upham asks the question, "What is it to be inwardly crucified? It is to have no desire, no purpose, no aim, but such as comes by Divine inspiration, or is attended by the Divine approbation. To be inwardly crucified, it is to cease to love Mammon in order that we may love God, to have no eye for the world's possessions, no ear for the world's applause, no tongue for the world's envious or useless conversation, no terror for the world's opposition. To be inwardly crucified is to be, among the things of the world a stranger and a pilgrim; separate from what is evil, sympathizing with what is good, but never with idolatrous attachment; seeing God in all things, and all things in God. To be inwardly crucified is, in the language of Tauler, to cease entirely from the life of self, to abandon equally what we see and what we possess, our power, our knowledge, our affections; so that the soul in regard to any action originating in itself is without life, without action, and without power, and receives its life, its action, and its power from God alone."

DEATH

Christ's death for sin is our death to it. There are many things to which we are dead in that death. We are dead to sin's penalty (Romans vi. 7), to sin's power (Romans vi. 2), to sin's presence (Romans vi. 7), to sin's practice (1. Peter ii. 24), to the law (Galatians ii. 19; Romans vii. 4), to self (11. Cor. v. 15), and to the world (Galatians ii. 20); and He died that we should live to Him (11. Cor. v. 15), and ultimately live with Him (11. Tim. ii. 12).

When Clerk Maxwell, the scientist, was asked what he thought was the greatest discovery of the nineteenth century, he replied that the greatest discovery that he knew of was that *"the Gramm machine is reversible."* The Gramm machine is for the producing of electricity; and it had been discovered that both power develops electricity, and electricity develops power; and that is what he meant when he referred to the fact that the machine is reversible. As powers develops electricity, and electricity power; so the death of Christ for us generates power over the cause of death—sin; and that victory over sin makes us appreciate more than ever His death for sin.

PASSION

Christ showed Himself alive after His *passion* (Acts i. 3). The word *"passion"* signifies intense suffering. It is translated *"vexed"* in Matthew xvii. 15; and *"felt"* in Acts xxviii. 5. The word is used to denote the sufferings of Christ on our account twenty times (Matthew xvi. 21; xvii. 12; Mark viii. 31; ix. 12; Luke ix. 22; xvii. 25; xxii. 15; xxiv. 26, 46; Acts iii. 18; xvii. 3; Hebrews ii. 9; v. 8; ix. 26; xiii. 12; 1. Pet. ii. 21, 23; iii. 18; iv. 1). We too are called to suffer for Him, since He has suffered for us. We are called, as Paul was, to suffer at the hands of the world for His sake (Acts ix. 16; Philippians i. 29; 1. Thessalonians ii. 14; 11. Thessalonians i. 5; 11. Timothy i. 12). We are also called to suffer wrongfully and thus follow in the steps of Christ (1. Peter ii. 19-21); not threatening our enemies (1. Peter ii. 23); and yet further, we are to suffer for righteousness sake and well doing (1. Peter iii. 14, 17); and in it all to commit ourselves in well doing to God (1. Peter iv. 19), remembering that suffering leads to the glory (1. Peter v. 10).

The suffering we may receive *from* men is nothing in comparison to the suffering of soul which the saint experiences on behalf *of* men. The sufferings of Christ make us feel with the Christ of the sufferings (1. Peter iv. 1). To arm ourselves with the same mind of Christ in suffering, we must know the sufferings of the mind which suffered. Henry Martin knew something of this when he said "I desire to burn out for my God." James Hannington had the same spirit when, in the face of tremendous opposition, he exclaimed, "I refuse to be disappointed; I will only praise." David Brainerd, burned with the same fire. He wrote in his journal: "I think my soul was never drawn out in intercession for others as it has been this night; I hardly ever so longed to live to God, and to be altogether devoted to Him; I wanted to wear out my life for Him. . . . I wrestled for the ingathering of souls, for multitudes of poor souls. I was in such an agony from sun half-an-hour high, till near dark, that I was all over sweat; but, oh! my dear Lord did sweat blood for such poor souls: I longed for more compassion."

SACRIFICE

Christ's sacrifice is alone and unique. He gave Himself "a sacrifice to God" (Eph. v. 2). That sacrifice ascended, like the burnt offering, as a sweet savour to God. It brought satisfaction and delight to Him. Christ was daily His delight before He came to earth; but on the earth, when He gave Himself up to death *"for us,"* God received a pleasure He had not received before.

We are now called, as the Holy Priesthood, to offer up spiritual sacrifices (1. Peter ii. 5). Some of those sacrifices are, the humble sacrifice of a broken heart (Psalm li. 17), the heart's sacrifice of adoring praise (Hebrews xiii. 15), the helpful sacrifice of doing good to others (Hebrews xiii. 16; Philippians iv. 18), the holy sacrifice of fellowship with others (Philippians ii. 17), and the living sacrifice of a wholly yielded body (Romans xii. 1).

Froude says of sacrifice, "In common things the law of sacrifice takes the form of positive duty. The law of Christian sacrifice goes beyond 'positive duty,' it spends itself, at its own cost out of love to Him Who spent Himself out for us. The Apostle uses two expressions which exemplify what kind of sacrifice is ignited by the flames of Calvary's sacrifice. He says, "I will gladly spend and be spent" (11. Corinthians xii. 15).

"Spend" means to incur cost, to expend, to consume. The word is used to denote the bankruptcy of the prodigal and the diseased woman: the one spending his all in riotous

living, and the other in paying doctors to rid her of her
malady (Luke xv. 14; Mark v. 26). The word is rendered
"Consume" in James iv. 3, and *"charges"* in Acts xxi. 24.

"Spent" means to be *exhausted*. It is the same as the
previous word, with the added preposition *"ek"*—*"ekda-
panao."* We might paraphrase the apostle's sentence, "I
would gladly spend all I have, and be spent out in doing it."

The seal of the London Missionary Society is an ox
standing between an altar and a plough, with the words,
"Ready for either." Sacrifice or service. The Calvary
moved man sacrifices himself in serving. "The Church is
Christian, as it is a continuous organ of the passion of
Christ." "We can never heal the needs we do not feel.
Tearless hearts can never be heralds of the Passion. We
must pity if we would redeem." We must perfect, by our
passion and sacrifice, the sacrifice and passion of our Lord.
The dying of our Lord in His members is to be constantly
effected by the indwelling Spirit.

"DELIVERED"

He was *delivered* for our offences" (Rom. iv. 25). Men
that have *"hazarded"* their lives (Acts xv. 26). Here is
another blood-drenched word. The word translated *"hazarded"* and *"delivered"* signifies to be absolutely given over.
There is more than risk suggested, the better word would
be abandoned. It is used to denote wicked men given over
by God to the sins to which they had given themselves.
When we give ourselves up, like the Lord, to obedience
unto death, we are effective servants as He proved to be.
An old proverb says, "We cannot have omelette without
breaking eggs." We cannot get anything whole without
something being broken. The aroma which filled the house

of Martha came from the broken box of spikenard and gave
pleasure to the contemplating Sufferer.   Judas spoke of
"waste" because he was *"a son of waste"* (the words *"waste"*
and *"perdition"* are one and the same in the Greek—John
xvii. 12; Matthew xxvi. 8).   When we give up our lives
to Him Who gave Himself for us, we give to some purpose.
The apostle speaks of the "form of doctrine which was delivered unto you" (Romans vi. 17).   The word *"delivered"*
is the same as occurs in Rom. iv. 25 and Acts xv. 26.
Rotherham renders the passage, "Ye become obedient out of
the heart into the mould of teaching into which ye were
delivered"; or as Moule, "To which ye were handed over."
The truth of the death of Christ is likened to a mould into
which believers have abandoned themselves like molten
metal, to be formed.   We often speak of holding truth, but
the true way is to let the truth hold us.   To be held by the
truth of Christ's death is to be fashioned like to Him Who
gave Himself up for us, which means we give ourselves
over in obedience to the will of God even as He did.

"LIFTED UP"

Christ spoke of His death as a *lifting up* (John iii. 14;
viii. 28; xii. 32, 34).   The word *"lifted up"* is also associated with the spiritual life.   It is rendered *"exalted"* in calling attention to the action of the Father in exalting Christ
to His own right hand (Acts ii. 33; v. 31), and the Lord
promises He will *"lift up"* (James iv. 10) and *"exalt"* those
who take the place of humility.   Christ took the lowest place
in death, and He now occupies, in consequence, the highest position in glory.   He stooped and conquered.   Those
who seek the highest place get the lowest, while those who
seek the lowest position are sooner or later given the high-

est one. The highest form of holiness is humility. Lowliness is the base of every virtue, and where it is not found holiness does not exist.

One thing of passing interest, in Christ's reference to the uplifted serpent in the wilderness is the word translated *"pole"* in Numbers xxi. 8, 9; it is the same as rendered *"Nissi"* in speaking of Jehovah our *Banner* (Exodus xvii. 15, margin). The word is frequently rendered *"banner"* (Psa. lx. 4; Isaiah xiii. 2), and *"ensign"* (Isaiah v. 26; xi. 10, 12; xviii. 3). The word means a sign or a signal. The author of *Wisdom* (xvi. 6) says, "A sign or signal of present salvation to the Israelites from the poison of the fiery serpents, and of the spiritual salvation from that old serpent, through Him Who was lifted upon the cross." The lifting up of Christ is God's sign of assurance that He will lift us up into all He has for us. Fellowship with the Christ in the lowliness of His death, is God's assurance that we shall have the livingness of His life. The deeper we sink into His death, the higher we rise into His life.

"MANIFESTED"

Christ in His death was the manifestation of the love and purpose of God (1. John iv. 9); hence we read, "He was *manifested*" to put away sin (Hebrews ix. 26, R. V.), and to destroy the works of the devil (1. John iii. 8). As He was the manifestation of God in all He did, so we are to manifest we belong to Him by not sinning (1. John iii. 10), by diligent heed to the things which He enjoins (1. Tim iv. 16), and by letting our blamelessness and harmlessness be seen by the world (Phil. ii. 15, R. V.). As Christ was the revelation of the Father in all He did and said, so we are to be the manifestation of Christ in all we do and say.

Shakespeare says—

> "To thy own self be true;
> And it must follow, as the night the day,
> Thou canst not then be false to any man."

I prefer to say—

> "To the Lord's death be true;
> And it must follow, as the night the day,
> Thou canst not then be false in anything."

Loyal-heartedness to His love will make us loving-hearted to our fellows. We love Him faithfully, as we serve others heartedly.

"BOUGHT"

"Bought with a price" is the Spirit's word as He reminds us to Whom we belong, and the price which Christ paid for us (1. Cor. vi. 20; vii. 23). The price which He paid was His own blood as the Elders affirm (Rev. v. 9, R. V.), and the answer to that price is our blood if needs be (1. John iii. 16). In the days of slavery an aged negro was put up for sale. A gentleman asked him, "My man, to whom do you belong?"

He answered, "My flesh, and bones, and blood belong to old Massa Carl, but my spirit am a free-born chield of God, bought by the precious blood of Christ."

Not only our spirit, but spirit, soul, and body belong to Him Who purchased us. The price He paid for us is above all price.

"What is the price of that picture?" said a lady to an artist's widow.

"That last work of my husband is beyond all price."

The price Christ paid for us cannot be priced, neither can we be bought by sin, the world, the flesh, and the devil, if we price ourselves at the price He paid. We were precious to Him so He paid His precious blood for us. And if we estimate ourselves at His price, no price can buy us from Him.

"CONSTRAINETH"

Christ in contemplating the fiery baptism of God's judgment against sin, with which He was to be immersed, said, "How am I straightened till it be accomplished?" (Luke xii. 50). The word *"sunecho,"* rendered *"straightened,"* means to compress, to hold together. It is used in speaking of a person *"taken"* with a sickness (Matthew iv. 24; Luke iv. 38), of one who is in the *"throng"* of a multitude (Luke viii. 45), of a man *"held"* forcibly by others (Luke xxii. 63), and of one in a *"strait"* between two things, who does not know which one to choose (Phil. i. 23). The word is further found in connection with Paul, once when he was *"pressed* in spirit" (Acts xviii. 5), and when he said, "The love of Christ *constraineth* us" (II. Cor. v. 14). Christ was pressed, thronged, impelled by the mighty love He had for us, hence, He went through the pressure of the winepress of God's judgment against our sin, and it is that fact of His love which holds us as in a master grip, and with which we grip Him and others.

There is a legend of an artist, who had in his picture a marvellous red tint. No other had learned the secret, and it died with him. After his death a red wound was discovered near his heart, and the secret of the wonderful color in his paintings was revealed. It was his heart's blood which gave his work the peculiar tint. The old legend tells a deep spiritual truth. Only heart's blood can give the hand of labor the needed touch of sympathy. Labor without love fades away like the cloud of mist before the sun, but love's labor is always in favor. The warmth of love makes the hand of work of sterling worth.

"REDEEM"

The practical purpose of Christ's redemptive work is, "that He might redeem us from all iniquity." The word *"lutroo,"* translated *"redeem"* in Titus ii. 14, means to ransom, and comes from *"lutron,"* which means a redemptive price by means of which anything is loosened from bondage, and *"lutron"* comes from the primary verb *"luo,"* which means to loosen, to dissolve, melt, put-off. *"Luo"* is rendered *"melt"* and *"dissolved"* in II. Peter iii. 10, 11; *"unloose"* in Mark i. 7; *"put off"* in Acts vii. 33; *"broken up"* in Acts xiii. 43; and *"destroy"* in I. John iii. 8. Christ died to break the power of sin, to destroy the works of the devil, to put off from us the old habits, and to dissolve the iniquity which once held us in its sway and way.

"Iniquity" is that from which Christ redeems. There are two words rendered "iniquity." One signifies unrighteousness, that is, anything which is not straight. It is translated *"iniquity"* and *"unrighteousness"* in II. Timothy ii. 19 and I. John i. 9. The other word which is used in the sentence we are considering, means lawlessness, the violation of law, and indicates man's self-will in opposition to God's will. We read of "the mystery of *iniquity*," or *"lawlessness"* (R. V.) in II. Thessalonians ii. 7. The essence of sin is self-will, the essence of holiness is doing God's will. To delight in God's will is to know God will delight in us. Christ died for us in carrying out God's will

in our salvation, and the outcome is, we die to our will, and
let Him work in us according to His good pleasure (Philippians ii. 13, R. V.).

"SANCTIFY"

Christ in His prayer for His disciples prays, "For their
sakes I sanctify myself" (John xvii. 19). Christ consecrated Himself in the consecration of His Father's will
that He might consecrate us to the Father. "For their
sakes" implies the sacrifice of Himself, and that sacrifice
was that believers might be sanctified in the truth. He gave
Himself for the Church that He might sanctify and cleanse
it, and He suffered without the gate that He might sanctify
the people with His own blood (Ephesians v. 26; Heb. xiii.
12). The iron ore is put into the furnace that the slag may
be separated from the useable and useful metal. Christ
was the holy fuel Who was consumed in the furnace of
God's holy purpose, that He might separate the refuse of
every unclean thing from us, and separate us, in the qualification of the Holy Spirit, to the Lord, that we might be
useable to Him and useful to others for Him. Separation
to the Holy One is to find the holiness, the love, the joy,
the grace, the power, the truth, of the Holy One, and for
the Holy One, to be separated to us.

"PERFECTED"

The goal of Christ's life was His death. One step short
of that end would have meant failure to Him, but He knew
He would be "perfected" (Luke xiii. 32), that He would
"finish" the work allotted to Him (John iv. 34), and He
was not disappointed in His faith, hence, He joyfully

exclaims "I have finished," "It is finished" (John xvii. 4; xix. 30). As a matter of grace, He has "perfected for ever" those who are sanctified (Hebrews x. 14). Now He desires we should have a perfect understanding in spiritual things (1. Corinthians xiv. 20, R. V., margin), a perfect standing in the will of God (Colossians iv. 12), a perfect stature in the Divine Life (Philippians iii. 15; Heb. v. 14; James i. 4), a perfect mastery over the tongue (James iii. 2), a perfect faith by corresponding work (James ii. 22), a perfect keeping of God's Word by our obedience (1. John ii. 4, 5), and a perfect love to God by loving each other (1. John iv. 12).

"Teleioo" and *"teleios,"* which are rendered "perfect" and "finished" in the above scriptures, signify completeness, reaching a goal, answering to a given end. Christ did that for us when He died on our account. All things that were written of Him were accomplished (John xix. 28), for He accomplished all the things which were written. All He commands us to do in His Word is possible, for He lives, since He died to carry out in us all He asks from us. He lives to purpose, when He lives in us to carry out His purpose.

"POURED OUT"

"He poured out His soul unto death" (Isaiah liii. 12) is the expressive declaration which reveals how much Christ gave in dying for us. The term, *"poured out,"* means, to demolish, to be destitute, to empty, to be made bare. It is rendered *"emptied"* in speaking of Rebekah emptying the water out of her pitcher (Genesis xxiv. 20), and *"rase"* (margin, "make bare") in describing the razing of a building to its foundation (Psalm cxxxvii. 7). Christ emptied Himself out for us that He might enrich us with the water of life; and He was razed to the ground that we might be found in the beautiful temple of His holiness.

The apostle, in writing to the Church at Philippi, says "If I be poured forth (margin) upon the sacrifice and service of your faith and joy" (Philippians ii. 17); and to his son, Timothy, he says, as he contemplates his death, "I am now ready to be poured out as a drink offering" (II. Tim. iv. 6, R. V., mar.). The reference is to the drink offering (Ex. xxix. 40, 41). The Greeks of old delighted to relate how Phidippides, having achieved great success in the great battle at Marathon, ran into Athens, and recounted the event, and closed his oration by exclaiming, "Rejoice ye, as we rejoice," and fell down dead. He out of love of country could do this, how much more should we be willing, out of love to Christ, to pour ourselves out for Him Who poured Himself out for us.

"THE PRINT OF THE NAILS"

"The print of the nails" (John xx. 25). The word translated "print" suggests a die, a stamp, or scar, and thus by analogy denotes a resemblance to that which made the impression. It is the word used in speaking of a sample, a figure. It is rendered *"figure"* in Rom. v. 14, *"pattern"* in Heb. viii. 5, and *"examples"* in I. Corinthians x. 6, 11. The nails' print proclaims the nails of our sin which made the print.

The same word frequently occurs in connection with the believer being an example of the power and blessing of the gospel. See Philippians iii. 17; I. Thessalonians i. 7; II. Thessalonians iii. 9; I. Timothy iv. 12; Titus ii. 7; I. Peter v. 3, where the words *"pattern"* and *"ensample"* are the same. The Holy Spirit also uses the word in Rom. vi. 17, where it is given *"form"* in calling attention to the "form of doctrine" to which the saints had been given up.

Bishop Hall gives the best interpretation of this thought —"Seest thou thy Saviour hanging on the cross? All hang there with Him, as a knight or burgess of Parliament voices his whole borough or country. The members take the same lot as the head. Every believer is a limb of that body; therefore, how can he but die with Him and in Him? That real union, then, which is betwixt Christ and us, makes the cross or any passion of Christ's ours; so the thorns pierced our heads, the scourges blooded our backs, the nails wounded our hands and feet, and the spear gored our sides and hearts; by virtue whereof we receive justification from our sins, and true mortification of our corruptions. Every believer, therefore, is dead already for his sins in his Saviour; he need not fear that he shall die again."

11

Service and Christ's Atonement

When the apostle Paul speaks of himself as a "servant of Jesus Christ" (Rom. i. 1; Titus i. 1), he uses the Greek word *doulos,* which means *"bondman,"* and is so rendered in Revelation vi. 15. The word comes from a root which means to bind, hence, signifies one who is in subjection to another; a slave, one who belongs to another. Believers in Christ are His slaves, for He has purchased them by His own blood, hence they are not their own. What was the secret underlying Paul's devotion to Christ and his endeavor to please God and not men? He himself answers the question, for he says, "If I yet pleased men I should not be the servant of Jesus Christ" (Gal. i. 10).

He recognized he was not his own, and therefore he could not do as he liked. The same thought is seen in Paul's prohibitive utterance, when he says to Timothy, "The servant of the Lord must not strive" (II. Tim. ii. 24). Why? Because he has no right. His lips belongs to another, and to that Other he is responsible not to wrangle, but to be gentle. It is this fact of His death which makes us say with Dora Greenwell:

> "——living, dying, let me bring
> My strength, my solace from this spring;
> That He who lives to be my King,
> Once died to be my Saviour."

Both in Christ's teaching and in the Spirit's ministry, believers are reminded they are the Lord's servants and His property, as the Apostle tersely says, "Whose I am and whom I serve" (Acts xxvii. 23).

I. *Recognition of the Lord, the basis of service.* "Ye serve the Lord Christ" (Col. iii. 24) is the practical word of the Apostle as he charges the servants to do all they do heartily, "as unto the Lord." To be influenced by the Lord as He directs in the word of His grace, is to have an influence for the Lord which is unmistakable in its blessing.

Among the knotty questions, which the Lord gave Job for his consideration was, "Canst thou bind the sweet influences of Pleiades?" (Job xxxviii. 31). To bind, or limit, the influence exerted by the cluster of stars known as the Pleiades is an impossibility. The same thing is true of the gracious influence which emanates from the cross. Men in their ignorance imagined at one time the earth was the center of the universe; then they thought the sun was, but bye and bye they discovered that the sun was moving round one of the stars in the cluster known as the Pleiades. "Vast as the distance is which separates our sun from his central group—a distance which is thirty-four million times greater than the distance between the sun and our earth—yet so tremendous is the force exerted by Alycone that it draws our system irresistibly around it at the rate of 422,000 miles a day, in an orbit which it will take many years to complete."

One other thing about the Pleiades, is the meaning of the word. The Chaldaic word *"chimah,"* literally means "a hinge, pivot, or axle," which moves round and moves other bodies along with it. Astronomers who knew nothing about the meaning of the word, by a series of independent calculations, have found out that the Pleiades is the axle round which the solar system revolves.

As the Pleiades influences the planetary system so the Lord Jesus in His wondrous death upon the cross, influences the believer in Himself. This may be seen in many ways, but I call attention to an incident in the life of John. When Christ appeared to John in Patmos, He made known to him by the revelation which was given to Him, that He was to "shew unto His servants things which must shortly come to pass;" and those servants are likened to "seven stars" which He holds in His hand. Before He explains the mystery of the seven stars, He speaks of Himself, as the "one who was dead," and who is "alive forevermore. The pierced One of Calvary holds His servants in His pierced hand, as He uses them in His service. As they feel the pressure of that dented hand, they are moved as the apostle was to devoted service, when he said, "The love of Christ constraineth me."

II. *Yieldingness to the Lord, the consecration of service.* "To whom ye yield yourselves *servants* to obey his *servants* ye are" (Rom. vi. 16)

In Christ's prayer for His people, He prays: "For their sakes I sanctify myself, that they also might be sanctified in the truth" (John xvii. 19). The word sanctify cannot mean to purify when applied to Christ, for He had no defilement to remove. The reference is to Christ's consecration of Himself in willing obedience to God in death, on our behalf; and not only so, but He gave Himself over to death on our account, that we might in turn be consecrated to Himself, and that He might communicate Himself to us; as Godet says, "The sanctification of every believer is nothing else than the communication which Jesus makes to him of His own sanctified person."

There are two things which are worthy of our special consideration, and these are the Consecrator, and the element of consecration. As to the latter Christ prays we may be sanctified "in the truth." Godet points out that there is no article in the Greek, and makes it read "in truth," that is, in a true way, in contrast to the Pharisaical pretentions and Levitical ceremonialism. But it seems to me that while this may be implied, there is a great deal more in the words. We must read them in the light of what goes before. Does not the "also" suggest an association? As Christ sanctified Himself to death, so in that fact of His death for us, we should live and move, for as another has said: "Christianity stands rooted in the divine act of reparation and retrieval. We are saved not of ourselves, but by the work of another. And our salvation consists in a continual union with Him who is the abiding Refuge and Healer and Restorer of His people. The Scriptures speak to us in many figures of that inward health and vitality which we recover in Him, who alone hath life in Himself, and who quickeneth whom He will."

Mark the words "our salvation consists in a continual union with Him," that is, I take it, the writer means the secret magnetic force of the Christian life is found in union with Him who gave Himself over to death for us. The thought in this case is not being delivered from the guilt of sin, nor being kept from its defilement, but it is in being lifted into a higher sphere altogether, namely, as Christ hallowed Himself in holy consecration to God for our benefit; so there should burn on the altar of our life, the holy fire of His passion, which shall inflame us in whole-hearted devotion to the will and service of God. This thought lifts us away from the low conception of the merely negative aspect of holiness, namely, separation from that which defiles, into the positive realm of whole-hearted consecration to God. In that realm, our spiritual comforts do not concern us, our soul's salvation does not trouble us, our spiritual progress does not occupy us, our work does not annoy us, our religious interests do not worry us, our brethren do not affront us, and our difficulties do not depress us. Our one attraction is the One who loved us and gave Himself for us, and we are so taken up with Him in holy activity in the will of God, that we exclaim with Rutherford, "Oh, to be a thousand fathoms deep in His love! He, He Himself is more excellent than heaven; for heaven is but a creature, and He is something more than a creature."

The other point is with reference to the Consecrator. We cannot say in the sense in which Christ could, "I sanctify myself." There is only one place in the whole of the New Testament where the Greek word *hagiazo* is used in relation to the believer, as suggesting he is the sanctifier, and that is in I. Peter iii. 15, where he is exhorted to sanctify Christ as Lord is his heart (R. V.), and there the thought is the recognition of the Lord as the dominant power, who is to regulate the life of the believer. In every other case where the Sanctifier is spoken of it is either the Father, the Son, the Holy Spirit, or the Word of God. The following Scriptures from the epistles will suffice to emphasise this fact:

"Sanctified by God the Father" (Jude 1).

"Christ loved the Church, that He might sanctify it" (Eph. v. 26).

"Sanctified in Christ Jesus" (I. Cor. i. 2).

"By the which will we are sanctified" (Heb. x. 10).

"Sanctify the people with His own blood" (Hebrews xiii. 12).

"Sanctified by the Word of God" (I. Tim. iv. 5).

"Sanctified by the Holy Ghost" (Romans xv. 16).

"The God of peace sanctify you" (I. Thess. v. 23).

Too many of God's children in their honest endeavor to be consecrated in this higher sense of the word, miss their purpose by their endeavoring. They need to learn the music and the meaning of what Frances Ridley Havergal says:

> "Church of God, belov'd and chosen,
>   Church of God, for whom Christ died,
> Claim thy gifts and praise the Giver!
>   "Ye are washed and sanctified!"
> Sanctified by God the Father,
>   And by Jesus Christ His Son,
> And by God the Holy Spirit,
>   Holy, holy Three in One.
>
> "By His will He sanctifieth,
>   By the Spirit's power within;
> By the loving hand that chast'neth,
>   Fruits of righteousness to win;
> By His truth, and by His promise,
>   By His Word, His Gift unpriced,
> By His blood, and by our union
>   With the risen life of Christ.
>
> "Holiness by faith in Jesus,
>   Not by effort of thine own,

Sin's dominion crushed and broken,
    By the power of grace alone;
God's own holiness within thee,
    His own beauty on thy brow,
This shall be thy pilgrim brightness
    This thy blessed portion now.

"He will sanctify thee wholly;
    Body, spirit, soul shall be
Blameless till thy Saviour's coming,
    In His glorious majesty:
He hath perfected for ever
    Those whom He hath sanctified;
Spotless, glorious and holy
    Is the Church, His chosen Bride."

A consecrated believer is never man-made, nor self-made, he is always a God-made one. One of Disraeli's admirers, in speaking of him to Mr. Bright, said, "You ought to give him credit for what he has accomplished, as he is a self-made man." "I know he is," retorted Mr. Bright, and "he adores his maker."

A believer is never a self-made man in the divine life, he must be God-made to be at all. Chalmers recognized this, when he spoke of the "expulsive power of a new affection." But Chalmers only touches half the truth, when he speaks of expulsion; what we want is, an inclusive and conclusive reign of a new inhabitant, for it is only as the Lord Himself dominates and directs every part of our nature, that we are truly consecrated by His consecrating personality to Himself..

III. *Carefulness before the Lord, the order of service.*
One of the highest appellations applied to Moses is, that he
was "the servant of God" (Rev. xv. 3).

The careful student of nature, and the prayerful student
of God's Word, are both impressed with one fact, namely,
that God is the God of Order.

"Order is Heaven's first law."

One illustration from His works, and one statement from
His Word will demonstrate this truth. The leaves on the
trees are arranged in such a way as to suit the nature and
circumstances of each of them; for instance, if we go into
an orchard and examine a young apple or cherry tree, we
shall find that the leaves are arranged round the stem spirally
in series of fives, the fifth leaf, or bud, standing directly
above the first. Why is it? The leaves being evenly dis-
tributed around the stem gives each a fair chance to get
the light and air which are requisite for its growth and
symmetry. Thus we find, not only "the heavens themselves,"
but the products of the earth

> "Observe degree, priority, and place,
> Insisture, course, proportion, season, form,
> Office and custom in all line of order."

When we turn to the pages of Holy Writ we find the
same carefulness—"See that thou make all things according
to the pattern shown thee in the mount," is the Lord's direction to Moses, regarding the tabernacle. Nothing was left
to the ingenuity of his brain, nor the concept of his thought,
nor the freak of his imagination, but everything was to be
"according to the pattern." The Apostle Paul recognises the
same thing with regard to Christ's death and resurrection.
There were many witnesses to the fact of Christ's resurrec-

tion, but Paul lays emphasis on it by saying it was "according to the Scriptures," for, as Godet points out, "The regimen 'according to the Scriptures,' has its importance; the divine testimony of the Scriptures is designedly placed above all the apostolic testimonies which are about to follow. The Scriptures had said the event would happen; the witnesses declare it has happened" (i. Cor. xv. i, etc.).

Another thing of importance to observe, is the prominence given to any stated truth. When Paul speaks of the death and resurrection of Christ, and uses the words "first of all" (I. Cor. xv. 3), he not only means first in the sense of coming first, but first in importance, as Godet remarks, "We need not give the word 'first' the temporal meaning; it is the fundamental importance of those one or two points which Paul wishes to characterise by the term." The soldiers in a royal procession come first in the order of the march, but the king is the first one as the personage of importance. That is the sense in which we must ever view Christ's death and resurrection. They can never take a secondary place. They must always be foremost and first. We call attention to Christ's death, to the fact, that "Christ died for our sins." This must ever be first in importance, because it is the most important truth of all. All truth is of importance, but there are certain truths which have a relative importance, and there are others which have an essential importance, even as the hub of the wheel is of essential importance to the wheel, because of the position it occupies, while the spokes are of importance because of their relative connection with the hub.

The servant of the Lord, ever treasures in his heart with jealous care, the truth of the Lord's death, for it is that death which has given him a gospel to preach, hence, he has a sacred trust to guard, as the Apostle indicates when he says, "The glorious gospel of the blessed God which was committed to my trust." (I. Tim. i. 11).

IV. *Resting in the Lord, the confidence of service.* Christ says "the servant is not greater than his Lord" (John xv. 20). Christ's greatness is seen in His lowliness. He always rested in the will of God, while about His work, and was empowered in the Spirit, as a result. The same holds good to us as we are in the place of lowly dependence on Christ. We need have no concern about our comforts, if we are occupied in His business.

The temple of Solomon was built on the place of sacrifice. When the Lord told Abraham to take his son Isaac, He told him to "go into the land of Moriah, and offer him there for a burnt offering upon one of the mountains" (Gen. xxii. 2) ; and it was in the same place Solomon erected the temple, for we read, "Solomon began to build the house of the Lord at Jerusalem in Mount Moriah,'" and it is not without significance that we further read, "where the Lord appeared unto David his father, in the place that David had prepared in the threshing-floor of Ornan, the Jebusite" (II. Chron. iii. 1). It was in that place David offered peace and burnt offerings upon the altar which he erected, and the Lord accepted his offerings, as was evidenced in the fire from heaven which fell upon them, and the devastating plague being stayed.

Reading these facts in the light of the New Testament, we can see their typical import, for as the temple was built on the place of Sacrifice, which had been consecrated by the substitutionary ram offered up in the stead of Isaac, and as the averting sacrifice upon which the fire of judgment fell, stayed the avenging stroke of Jehovah upon Israel; so

Christ's death in all its glorious sufficiency, is the basis upon which the believer rests for his soul's salvation; the plan which shapes him as a holy temple for the Lord's occupancy; and the source of all service.

The Greek preposition *epi* when it occurs with the dative implies a resting in, and a conjunction with, a thing or person. Its use will illustrate this. It is used in speaking of a person lying *"in"* a bed, people sitting *"upon"* the grass, one stone resting *"upon"* another, Christ sitting *"upon"* an ass, acting *"at"* Christ's direction, Christ resting *"on"* a well, a stone lying *"upon"* a tomb's entrance, and of persons being saved from drowning by floating *"on"* boards (Mark ii. 4; vi. 39; xiii. 2; xi. 7; Luke v. 5; John iv. 6; xi. 38; Acts xxvii. 44). The meaning of the word is thus aptly illustrated by its use. This very preposition is used again and again in speaking of the believer's trust in the Lord. Thus Mary confesses she rejoices *"in"* God, her Saviour" (Luke I. 47); Peter declares that *"through* faith in" the "name" of Jesus brought wholeness to the lame man (Acts iii. 16); Isaiah proclaims Christ as the One *"in"* whom the Gentiles shall trust to their blessing (Rom. xv. 12); Paul makes known the basis of the Church in speaking of it as resting *"upon* the foundation of the apostles and prophets, Jesus Christ Himself being the Chief Corner Stone" (Eph. ii. 20); those who "believe *on"* Christ obtain everlasting life (I. Tim. i. 16); and whoso "believeth *on* Him shall not be confounded" (I. Pet. ii. 6). These Scriptures prove beyond all question, to faith, that Christ in His finished work is the only resting place for the soul's salvation, and the only basis of peace, yea, the starting point and the stopping place of all things in the divine life. Suppose we weave the above illustrative Scriptures into the fact of Christ's death as the resting place of the believer's faith and service. He is the bed of rest, where we can lie to our heart's ease; He is the place of supply where we can feed to our heart's content; He is the upholder in the place of God's building; He is the sustainer as we journey in life's way: He is the sure success in the carrying out of His direction; He is the heart's refresher when thirsty in God's work; He is the hider of death's corruption and the life of our heart's love; and He is the sure place in which to rest, when we are occupied about His business.

V. *Looking to the Lord, the attractibility of service.* Christ to benefit us "took the form of a servant," namely, a slave (Phil. ii. 7). He took seven downward steps in serving us, and God caused Him to have seven corresponding steps of exaltation, as will be seen in the following contrast (Phil. ii. 6-11):

1. "Made Himself of no reputation."
2. "Took upon Him the form of a servant."
3. "Made in the likeness of men."
4. "Being found in fashion as a man."
5. "He humbled Himself."
6. "Became obedient unto death."

1. "God hath highly exalted Him."
2. "Given Him a name above every name."
3. "At the Name of Jesus every knee should bow."
4. Heaven acknowledges Him — "Things in heaven."
5. All earth owns Him— "Things in earth."
6. Hell submits to Him— "Things under the earth."

7. "The Death of the cross." | 7. "Every tongue" confesses He "is Lord to the glory of God the Father."

Christ is the Perfect Pattern of lowly service, and we are exhorted to let the mind that was in Him to be in us (Phil. ii. 5). How can we obtain that mind? By looking to Him, that He may be the mind to think, and act, in and through us.

Thomson in addressing nature, which perhaps is an ambiguous way of speaking to God, says:

"O, Nature,
Enrich me with the knowledge of thy works;
Snatch me to heaven."

The thought in the poet's mind evidently is this, heaven's truths are found in earth's secrets. We cannot find God by searching in the haunts of nature, but having found Him in Christ, we may find illustrations of His grace and love in all His works, for as Young reminds us:

"The course of nature is the art of God."

The common daisy on the roadside has a voice to us, if we will but listen. We have to say to it, as Wordsworth did long since:

"Bright flower! whose home is everywhere.
Bold in maternal Nature's care,
And all the long year through, the heir
Of joy or sorrow.
Methinks that there abides in thee
Some concord with humanity,
Given to no other flower I see
The forest through!

One thing about the daisy is its responsiveness to the sun and to no other light. In the evening hour the daisy closes its petals around its heart. The lamp-lighter lights the gas lamps, and the gas light plays upon the daisy in its bed of green, but it opens not. The moon rises and pours her silvery rays upon the humble flower of earth, and floods all around with her beautiful sheen; but there is no response on the part of her whose "cheek is tipped with a blush." The moon sets and one by one the stars shine out from the canopy of heaven, but still there is no response on the part of her, who is of "silver crest and golden eye." The morning light comes, and the warm touch of the sun's beams kisses the flower of "snawie bosom sunward spread," and immediately, as Burns says, "thou lifts thine unassuming head." The sunlight did what no other light could do. Why? "Because the daisy found in the sunshine the stimulus of its vital action—the food which it assimilated," and by means of which it was able to grow the bright colors which adorned it, and made it what it was. The light of the sun was its life.

What is true of the daisy in the natural world is infinitely more so in the spiritual realm of grace. The one object which attracts the saint is the Christ of Calvary. In the darkness of His cross we find the light of heaven. In the bitterness of His woe we receive the joy of His salvation. In the poverty of His humiliation we discover the riches of His love. Christ's death is the death of sin, the begeter of love, the stimulus to faith, the gladness of hope, the ardor of zeal, the inspirer in service, and the fervor of testimony, which makes us say, "My Beloved is white and ruddy." White in His spotless character, and ruddy in His all-glorious death. Then with new buoyancy and increased zest, we exclaim, "This is my Beloved, and this is my Friend." "Whom have I in heaven but Thee, and there is none on earth I desire beside Thee."

"Looking unto Jesus . . . who . . . endured the cross" (Heb. xii. 2) is the attitude of the believer's life, in order to discover His attractiveness. Christ is the one attraction of the child of God, but He does not become this by a mere casual glance. There must be intensity of gaze. This is not only implied by the verb used, but also by the preposition. The meaning of the word translated *"unto"* might be equally rendered *"into."* It is so given in speaking of the angels who desired to "look *into*" the things relating to Christ's sufferings and glory which were penned by the Holy Spirit in the sacred writings (I. Peter i. 12). The same thought is found in James i. 25, where we are exhorted to look *"into* the perfect law of liberty." So that the sentence might with equal force, yea, be better rendered by, "looking *into* Jesus." Not merely *"at"* Jesus as the astronomer looks at a star by means of a telescope, but looking *"into"* Him as the scientist looks into the organism of an insect by means of a powerful microscope, which enables him to see every particle of its being.

VI. *Acting from the Lord, the power of service.* When we act at His bidding we are sure of His blessings. "If I yet pleased men, I should not be the servant of Christ" Gal. i. 10), affirms the apostle. He knew the Lord and the Lord knew His servant. The centurion was a man under authority, and therefore he could say to his servant, "Do this," and he did it (Matt. 8. 9). Being a man under authority he had authority. The same holds good in the service of Christ, when we act from Him in obedience to

His bidding, we may be assured we shall have the power of His presence to command others. It was the Christ who had died on Calvary, who had authority to command His disciples to go and preach the Gospel, and that authority had been "given unto" Him because He had previously carried out the command of the Father to die for the sheep. (Compare Matt. xxviii. 18, 19, and John x. 18, remembering the word *"power,"* in each Scriptures signifies author‧ity, and not strength, namely, the right to act.)

The consciousness of the Lord's presence and commission has ever made His servants faithful and fearless. The disciples at Pentecost were conscious of the Christ of Calvary, risen from the dead, hence, they feared not the face of men. The marred face of the Saviour made the fearless faces of His servants. Bloody Nero could not burn out the fires ignited by the cross; the cruel Inquisition could not daunt those who knew the Sufferer of Calvary; the Diet of Worms could not deter the faithful Martin Luther, for the thesis of the Gospel of blood, was more powerful than the Pope's bull; the devoted covenanters of Scotland were hunted from house and home, and found shelter in the mists of the mountains, for they knew the "Hind of the morning" who was hunted by the wolves of hell and nestled to His bleeding side; the fires of Oxford burned the bodies of Ridley and Latimer, but those fires only brought them into fellowship with Christ and His sufferings; and the saintly Samuel Rutherford immured in Aberdeen prison found the "durance vile" a means of communion with His Lord, as he said, "Welcome, welcome cross of Christ, if Christ be with it!"

VII. *Love to Christ, the spring of service.* "By love serve one another" (Gal. v. 13). The word "serve" signifies to serve as a slave. Not to serve slavishly, that is, in a way which indicates the service is irksome, but serve as a slave because impelled by love, for as the word for servant indicates the bondage of a slave, so when applied to a child of God it speaks of loving devotion. This is the spirit of Him, who came not to be ministered unto, but to minister and to give His life as a ransom for many.

There is a beautiful illustration of this in the Old Testament in the case of the slave who was freed in the year of jubilee, and who would not accept his freedom because he loved his master so well. When he thus declared himself, the master took his servant, and with an awl bored his ear and transfixed him to the doorpost, and he was declared to be his servant forever (Ex. xxi. 1-6). The bored ear was a declaration of love, and a seal of accepted service, and the man being fixed for the moment to the doorpost, proclaimed his consecration to the master of the house, and the absolute right of the master over the servant. The pierced ear was a mark of his love. There is an undoubted reference to this ordinance when Christ in speaking of Himself in relation to His sacrificial work, says, "Mine ear hast Thou opened" (Ps. xl. 6). The word "opened," as the margin indicates, should be *"digged,"* and as Newberry says, *"digged,* or *bored, cahrithah* from *cahrah,* to dig. The word is rendered *"digged"* in speaking of Isaac's servants who *"digged* a well" (Gen. xxvi. 25); *"bought,"* when Jehovah speaks of buying a woman (Hosea iii. 2); *"prepared"* and *"make a banquet"* in the sense of preparing a feast (2 Kings vi. 23; Job xli. 6); and the word is translated *"pierce,"* where the Spirit in the prophetic word foretells the piercing of the hands and feet of Christ (Ps. xxii. 16). The Holy Spirit takes the passage of Ps.

xl. 6, and directly applies it to Christ's incarnation, service, and substitutionary work, and makes Him say, "A body hast Thou prepared me" (Heb. x. 6). The context shows, the body was prepared to be a sacrificial victim. Christ's loving service and devoted consecration to the will of God are indicated in His saying, as He Himself says, "The Lord God hath opened mine ear, and I was not rebellious" Isaiah 1. 5).

Christ's devotion even to the death, in love for us, is the inspiring cause of our devotion to Him. No hardship is too great, no trial is too severe, no suffering is too intense, no task is too difficult, no load is too great, no cross is too heavy, and no loss is too large, when viewed in the light of the loss He sustained, the cross He carried, the load He bore, the task He undertook, the suffering He endured, and the hardship which weighted Him, when

"In my place condemned He stood."

James Chalmers recognised this, when he proclaimed after long years of difficulty and hardship, his unalterable choice, in the following words, "I recall the twenty-one years, give me back all its experience, give me its shipwrecks, give me its standings in the face of death, give it me surrounded with savages and clubs, give it me back again with spears flying about me, with the club knocking me to the ground—give it me back, and I will still be a missionary!"

VIII. *Equipment by the Lord, the supply of service.* When the Lord called His servants together, He gave to each of His servants a pound, that they might trade in His absence, and said, "Trade till I come (Luke xix. 13-15). The servant who gained ten pounds by his faithful trading recognised that the capital which was given him was the cause of his gain, as John Trapp quaintly makes him say, "Lord, Thy pound and not my pains hath gained ten pounds." The pound evidently represents the Gospel, with which every servant is responsible to trade, since the Lord has entrusted it to us. The apostle frequently refers to what had been entrusted to him and others (II. Cor. v. 19; I. Tim. vi. 20; II. Tim. i. 12, R. V. M.), and that Gospel is not only seed for the sower, but bread for the eater (Isaiah lv. 10, 11; 2 Tim: ii. 6), hence, Christ's death is the medium of the Divine supply, for His flesh and blood are "meat indeed" (John vi. 53-56). Ignatius recognised this when He said, "I have no delight in corruptible food, nor in the pleasures of this life. I desire the Bread of God, the Heavenly Bread, the Bread of Life, which is the flesh of Jesus Christ, the Son of God; and I desire the Drink of God, namely, His blood, which is incorruptible love and eternal life."

As it was from the smitten rock in the wilderness the water gushed forth to meet the need of famished Israel; so it is from the smitten Christ the blessing of divine grace flows to us. "Thou shalt smite the rock" (Ex. xvii. 6), was the direction which the Lord gave to Moses. We refer to the direction because the word *"nakah"* rendered *"smite,"* is found in connection with Christ as the Smitten One. The following instances where the word is found will be of suggestive interest: "They persecuted Him, whom Thou hast *smitten"* (Ps. lxix. 26). *"Smite* the Shepherd" (Zech. xiii. 7). "I gave My back to the *"smiters"* (Is. l. 6). "My heart is *smitten"* (Ps. cii. 4). "I was *wounded"* (Zech. xiii. 6). *"Smitten* of God" (Is. liii. 4).

Christ was smitten on our account, that we might not be smitten for our sins. Now the promise comes to us in consequence, "The sun shall not smite thee" (Ps. cxxi. 6).

Right through the Scriptures we find the same sequence
of thought. He is smitten, then we are sheltered. The as-
cending smoke of Noah's sacrifice brings forth the promise
that the Lord will not again destroy the earth with water
(Gen. viii. 21). The blood of the paschal Lamb protecting Israel in Egypt, is followed by Israel's deliverance from
Egypt (Ex. xii. 23, 51). The tree cut down sweetens the
bitter water of Marah, then the Israelites drink to their re-
freshment and rest (Ex. xv. 26). The uplifted serpent in
the wilderness brings life to the looking Israelite, then Israel can pitch their tents towards the sun-rising (Num. xxi.
9-11). The corn of wheat falls into the ground and dies,
then there follows the "much fruit" of blessing (John xii.
24). The foundation is laid, then the building is erected
(I. Cor. iii. 11, 12) ; and the Lamb must be slain for us,
before we can have the glory with Him, for it was after He
said, "I have finished the work," that He prayed, "I will
that they whom Thou hast given Me, be with Me, where I
am that they may behold My glory."

Pentecost follows the Passover, and it is because of the
Passover of Christ's death that there is the Pentecost of
the Spirit's power and presence. The dying words of
Adolphe Monod sum up the whole truth in its relative importance, he said, "All in Christ, by the Holy Spirit, for the
glory of God. All else is nothing." "By the Holy Spirit,"
for He it is who convinces of sin, imparts the new life, enables us to trust in Christ, unites us to Him, leads by His
word, inspires by His praying, inflames by His love, effect-
ually works by His power, strengthens by His grace, sanc-
tifies by His truth, preserves by His power, and keeps us
for the Lord's glory.

12

The Glory and Christ's Atonement

What is glory? The excellence of anything in display. The pearl in the oyster shell is none the less a pearl in the depths of the sea, but its excellence is not seen till it is set in the ring. The glory of Solomon's kingly splendour and the magnificence of his surroundings took all the spirit out of the Queen of Sheba (II. Chron. ix. 4), but the glory of the common lily of the East outshines the splendour of his retinue and regality (Matt. vi. 28, 29).

The glory of God's handiwork shews forth the excellence of God's artistic skill (Ps. xix. 1); the glory of His law proclaims the excellence of His righteousness (II. Cor. iii. 9); the glory of His holiness unfolds the excellence of His nature (John xii. 41); the glory of His grace declares the favour of His love (Eph. i. 6, 12, 14); the glory of His work speaks of the excellence of His power (John ii. 11; xi. 40); the glory of His gospel reveals the light of the knowledge of God in the face of Jesus Christ (II. Cor. iv. 6); and the glory of His heaven is the slain Lamb of Calvary (Rev. xxi. 11, 23).

The bliss and the blessedness of the future state are secured by the blood of the Lamb. The Lamb, as such, in the livingness of His death, is said to be the light of the New Jerusalem. We are told "the glory of God did lighten it," and then the explanatory sentence follows, "And the Lamb is the light thereof" (Rev. xxi. 23). The association of Calvary's blood with heaven's bliss proclaims one fact, namely, that the Christ of the glory has secured

the glory of the Christ, because of the substitutionary act
of His blood-shedding on the cross. This is emphasized by
the connection between the blood and the glory as revealed
in the Book of the Revelation. There are four references
to the blood in that Book, and in three out of the four the
blood is connected with the glory. The words speak for
themselves. "Unto Him that loved us, and washed us
from our sins in His own blood and made us kings and
priests unto God" (Rev. i. 5, 6). Loved, loosed, and lifted,
are the thoughts embodied in these words. *"Loved"*: the
word is in the present tense, as the R.V. indicates—"loveth."
His love is like the sun, constant in its shining, healing in its
warmth, and powerful in its influence. *"Loosed"*: The
word "washed" is rendered "loosed" in the R.V. The Greek
"louo" signifies to clear or to cleanse. The blood of Christ
clears the conscience from the penalty of sin and the heart
from the pollution of sin, even as the cleansed garment is
freed from the dirt which soiled it. *"Lifted"*: "Made us
kings and priests," or, more correctly, "made us a kingdom
of priests." The thought embodied expresses more than
the present priesthood of believers. It points on to their
reign with Christ, for as He will sit as a Priest-King on
His throne (Zech. vi. 13), so they will be royal also in
their priestly kingship and and their kingly priesthood.

The song of the living creatures and the four and twenty
elders is peculiar and "new," for whether we take the song
to refer to themselves or to the company "out of every
kindred," the thought is, the redeemed ones are in the
glory of the Lamb, because they have been redeemed to
God by His blood" (Rev. v. 9). The same thought is
expressed in Revelation vii. 14, where the saved host out
of the Great Tribulation are said to stand before the throne
of God and of the Lamb, because they "washed their robes

and made them white in the blood of the Lamb." The above Scriptures are sufficient to prove the right to the glory is secured by the night of the cross (Rev. xxii. 14, R.V.). Let us look at a few points in particular to prove the truth in general.

I. A TYPICAL FORECAST

On the Great Day of Atonement there was a five-fold atonement made. First atonement was made by the priest, for himself and his home; second, for the people; third, for the holy place; fourth, for the tabernacle; and fifth, for the altar (Lev. xvi. 6, 15, 16, 17, 18). The priest, making an atonement for himself and his house is typical of Christ in His identification with His own, standing with them in the desert of their sin, giving to God satisfaction on their behalf, and covering them in the merit of His person and work. There is no doubt a reference to this in the words, "We see Jesus . . . for the suffering of death, crowned with glory and honour: that He by the grace of God should taste death for every man. For it became Him, for whom are all things, and by whom are all things, in bringing many sons unto glory, to make the Captain of their salvation perfect through sufferings" (Heb. ii. 9, 10). The death of the Son was essential to bring the sons into the divinity of the glory. But since He has gone into the woe of our death, we shall surely enter into the welcome of His glory.

Second. The high priest made atonement for the nation; that is, for the nation of Israel. There is one nation that is the special object of God's regard. That nation is not reckoned among the nations (Num. xxiii. 9), and is specially called His "peculiar treasure" (Exo. xix. 5). There

are special promises given to Israel, and these promises
relate to Abraham regarding the land (Gen. xvii. 4-8), and
to David in connection with the throne (ii. Sam. vii. 12).
But these promises centralize in the Christ, the promised
Seed (Gen. xii. 3, 7; Gal. iii. 16), the Babe of Bethlehem
(Luke i. 32, 33), the Lord of Calvary. He came to
"redeem them who were under the law" (Gal. iv. 5), that
they who were under the law might know their sins were
atoned for by His blood, for His death is retrospective in
its benefit as well as prospective in its blessing, hence the
word declares that God hath set Him forth "through faith
in His blood, to declare His righteousness for the passing
over of the sins done aforetime" (Rom. iii. 25, R.V.). The
same one who died for Israel is the One who is coming to
Israel with blessing. When the nation looks upon Him,
they behold Him as the Pierced One, as we read in Zechariah xii. 10. "They shall look upon Me whom they have
pierced," and in the Book of the Revelation the same
thought is emphasized when Christ is described in His
coming glory—"Behold He cometh with clouds and every
eye shall see Him, and them also who pierced Him" (Rev.
i. 7). Israel's restoration to Palestine (Jer. xxxii. 37-42),
the reoccupancy of David's throne (Exe. xxxvii. 24), the
redivision of the land (Eze. xlviii.), the reunion of Judah
and Israel (Eze. xxxvii. 15-21), the glory of Jerusalem
(Isaiah i. 26: Zech: viii), the salvation of Israel (Eze.
xxxvi. 23-29), and the glory of God as the centre of His
earthly glory (Eze. xliii. 1-7), are all secured by the Christ
of Calvary. The crowning proof of this is the reintro-
duction of the sacrifices in the millennium, but they will be,
as the Lord's Supper is with us, commemorative of the
death of Christ, instead of being typical (Eze. xlvi. 4-7,
11-15).

Third. Atonement had to be made for the holy place (Lev. xvi. 16). The holy place is typical of the heavens. Even the heaven of God's presence could only be entered by means of Christ's blood (Heb. ix. 12), but the heaven of the heavenly places, having been polluted by the presence of the evil one, must be cleansed by the blood, and having been cleansed by the casting down of Satan, the redeemed will be caught up to meet Christ in the air (Rev. xii. 9-12; 1. Thes. iv. 17).

Fourth. Atonement was made for the tabernacle (Lev. xvi. 16). The tabernacle is associated with the earth, hence, Christ, tabernacled in human flesh. The earth cursed by sin has been sanctified by the blood of its Creator being shed upon it. There is a good time coming when the curse will be removed from the earth. "Instead of the thorn shall come up the myrtle tree; and it shall be to the LORD for a Name, for an everlasting sign that shall not be cut off" (Isa. lv. 13). Besides this, the desert places of the earth shall become productive, as we read in Isa. xxxv. 1— "The wilderness and the solitary place shall be glad for them, and the desert shall rejoice and blossom as the rose." Yea, "the earth shall yield her increase" (Ps. lxvii. 6). Instead of bad seasons and unprofitable crops, there shall be abundance and prosperity. As Dr. A. J. Gordon says, "Earth will then lay off her soiled week-day garb and put on her Sabbath dress, and, with her singing robes about her, take up again that anthem which was heard when the sons of God shouted for joy. The beauty of holiness and the eternal harmony of redemption must be displayed where the dishonor of sin has been most visible. Therefore this globe which has so long served for fallen man, will now serve for man upraised; yea, more, as Anselm says: 'The whole earth, which carried in its lap the body of the Lord, will be a paradise.' "

Fifth.   Atonement was made for the altar (Lev. xvi. 18). This was the altar of the burnt offering, where the animals were slain, and its being sprinkled with the blood may be typical of the association between the animal creation and the blessing it shall have because of redemption.   God sent the LORD Jesus in suffering once, but He is going to send Him back again, that He may fulfil the prophecy which speaks of the restitution of all things (Amos ix. 11-15; Acts iii. 21).   The restitution is guaranteed by Christ's death, for He died "to reconcile all things to Himself, by Him, whether they be things in earth or things in heaven" (Col. i. 20).

The present condition of creation is most graphically described in Romans viii. 22—"The whole creation groaneth and travaileth in pain together until now."   We have only to listen with attentive ears to find that a deep-drawn sigh is continually going up to the Lord from the animal creation, as Goethe says, "Often have I had the sensation as if Nature, in wailing sadness, entreated something of me, so that not to understand what she longed for cut me to the heart."   But besides the sighing, there is the expectation of the animal creation, yea, of all creation.   "For the earnest expectation of the creation waiteth for the revealing of the sons of God (Rom. viii. 19, R.V.).   The attitude of creation is most expressive, as Godet says, "A sculptor of any imagination and genius might carve a statue of Hope from it."   The picture is this: "Nature, an unwilling slave to vanity and corruption, stands, impatient of her bonds, with uplifted head, scanning with longing eyes the distant point of the horizon from which she looks for help, her hands outstretched to grasp and welcome the redemption into freedom and perfection which she yearns for and confidently expects."

II.   A PROPHETIC STATEMENT

In looking at many Old Testament prophecies, they are like the Alps of the Bernese Oberland—they seem to be a mass of mountain range in the distance; but when the tourist stands on the top of the Faulhorn, or goes over the Wengen Alp, or looks at the panoramic view at Murren, he sees many more peaks; so as we study the Old Testament prophecies relating to Christ, in the distance they seem to be the mountain peak of one event, but when we come nearer, in the course of time, we discover there is more than one peak. There is the black peak of His death and there is the snow-capped peak of His glory. This is brought out in that descriptive and detailed chapter of the sufferings of Christ—Is. liii. In that portion of Holy Writ there is the emphatic note of coming glory. The Spirit has specially emphasized this in the "He shalls" of Isaiah lii. 14, liii. The association will be marked if we note the following complete sentences:

"Visage marred" . . . "He shall sprinkle many nations" (Is. lii. 14). The sprinkling of many nations evidently refers to the benefit which Christ shall confer upon them because of His death, for the word "sprinkle" means to "besprinkle in expiation," as Aaron on the day of atonement sprinkled the blood on and before the mercy seat in making an atonement for the sins of the people. The visage marred Man becomes the Benefactor to the nations of the earth.

"It pleased JEHOVAH to bruise Him" . . . *He shall* see His seed" (Isa. liii. 10).

His bruising meant a great deal to Him, as well as to JEHOVAH and us. Because of that bruising He shall see His seed, born and brought in, educated and brought up, supported and brought through and glorified and brought home.

"Thou shalt make His soul an offering for sin" . . . *"He shall* prolong His day" (Isa. liii. 10).

Seemingly cut off by an untimely death, He shall have a prolonged honour conferred upon Him. As He was made sin for others, so His prolonged glory shall be shared by the redeemed.

"He shall bear their iniquities . . . *He shall* see of the travail of His soul and *shall* be satisfied" (Isa. liii. 11).

He travailed in pain when the load of our guilt was pressing Him sore, and He shall surely be satisfied with the result of His anguish, even as the mother is satisfied with the child which cost her the throes of suffering.

"Because He hath poured out His soul unto death . . . *He shall* take the spoil from the strong" (Isa. liii. 12).

Lowth's translation as given above declares Christ's victory over the power of evil. He did not, and will not, "share the spoil with the strong," but He has taken the spoil from the strong, and He will continue going forth to conquer, till the hosts of hell are completely overthrown and the great enemy is consigned to the lake of fire.

His sufferings were a necessity for our salvation and also for His glory and ours, as He Himself said, "Ought not Christ to have suffered . . . and to enter into His glory."

III. A DOUBLE EVENT

"And as it is appointed unto men once to die, but after this the judgment; so Christ was once offered to bear the sins of many; and unto them that look for Him shall He appear the second time without sin unto salvation" (Heb. ix. 27, 28). The forcefulness of these words is found in the pivot words "as" and "so." The common and deserved lot of humanity is death because of sin and after death the judgment, but Christ has died the death and borne the judgment for the believer, so that he is looking for neither death nor judgment, but the coming of the LORD. Indirectly there is a reference to the high priest making atonement for the people on the great day of atonement, and then coming out in his robes of glory and beauty to bless them. The past event of Christ's being offered for sins and the promise of His future coming are intimately connected. They are the Alpha and Omega of the Gospel; they are the foundation and roof of truth; they are the starting-point and terminus of revelation; they are the base and topstone of God's purpose; they are the cause and effect of love's provision; they are the earnest and full payment of eternal life; and they are the ground and outcome of grace, for what is grace but glory in the bud, and what is glory but grace in its fulness.

IV. A TRIPLE BLESSING

God in the wisdom and love of His grace has made Christ to be to us "Righteousness, Sanctification, and Redemption" (I. Cor. i. 30, R.V.). Righteousness is associated with Christ's work on the cross, when He by one righteous act fully met all the claims of God's law (Rom. v. 18), and now believers are reckoned righteous (Rom. iv. 3-10, 24) in Him who is the Righteousness of God (II. Cor. v. 21). Righteousness is conformity to God's claim as the Righteous One. As there were two ways by which the Israelite could conform to God's law, namely, by perfect obedience to it, or by dying for his disobedience, so Christ as our Representative has proved by His perfect obedience to God His intrinsic perfection, and by dying for us, His complete answer for sin's condemnation.

"Sanctification" is conformity to God's nature, for He is holy. The word "sanctification" is rendered "holiness" in Romans vi. 22, in the sentence, "Your fruit unto holiness." Holiness in a general sense means that which is set apart from a common to a sacred use, hence, believers are "sanctified in Christ Jesus" (1. Cor. i. 2), as being set apart to God in their identification with Him. Christ is also set apart to us in God's act of reckoning grace. Therefore the Holiness of Christ is reckoned to us and speaks of what He is to us in the livingness of His Divine personality as our Representative at God's right hand. As the words "HOLINESS TO THE LORD" were upon the mitre of the high priest, that the children of Israel might always be accepted before the LORD (Exo. xxviii. 36-38), so Christ ever lives for us (Heb. vii. 25). What He is for us, is imputed to us for our benefit, and what He can be in us, is imparted to us for our blessing.

"Redemption" is prospective in its application, for it forecasts the time when salvation will be consummated in the perfection of the glorified body. As the vine is composed of three principal parts—root, branches, and fruit—so redemption is threefold. There is deliverance from the curse and condemnation of sin through faith in Him, who died for us (Eph. i. 7); there is release from the iniquity and self-will of sin, and separation to holiness of life and labour through fellowship with Christ in the power of the Spirit (Titus ii. 14); and there will be freedom from the presence of sin and likeness to Christ's glorified body, when

He returns, hence, "we are waiting for the adoption, the redemption of our body" (Rom. viii. 23). This threefold redemption may be illustrated in the following simple way: A balloon is a thing which is made in a pear shape by sewing a number of pieces of silk together, which, when finished, is inflated, and when ready to ascend is released from the ropes which keep it down to earth. Christ by His work on the cross has made us what we are, even as the skilled mechanic makes the balloon; Christ fills us by His Spirit and thus occupies the sphere of our being, even as the gas fills the balloon, and thus makes the pieces of combined silk what they were not before; and Christ when He comes again will release us from the earth condition of a body humiliated by sin, and cause us to rise to the realm of the glorified state, even as the balloon soars above the earth when released.

Christ as our "Righteousness" secures our redemption; Christ as our "Holiness" endows us with all the blessings of redemption, and Christ as our "Redemption" consummates our salvation. The first takes us back to the smitten rock of Calvary, the second takes us up to the throne of grace and acceptance, and the third ushers us into the holiest of His glorious presence. The first makes faith sing, "The past is all answered for"; the second causes love to say, "The present is all provided for"; and the third thrills hope with expectant joy, for she says, "The future is all secured." The first proclaims the Good Shepherd dying, the second announces the Great Shepherd living, and the third says, "The Chief Shepherd is coming."

V. A COMFORTING WORD

The saints at Thessalonica were haunted with the fear that their loved ones who had fallen asleep in Christ would be left behind when He came in His kingdom and glory, therefore the Holy Spirit assures them through Paul that death does not sever their oneness with the Lord, and lays it down as an article of faith that "if," or since, "we believe that Jesus died and rose again, even so them also who sleep in Jesus will God bring with Him" (1. Thess. iv. 14). The emphasis undoubtedly is on the sentences, "Jesus died and rose again" and "In Jesus." The last sentence should be "By Jesus," for it is the preposition *dia*, which, when it occurs with the genitive, signifies an active agent, and should therefore be rendered "By means of Jesus." The sentence may be punctuated as follows: "Them also who sleep, by means of Jesus will God bring with Him." Thus the sleeping ones do not sleep by means of Jesus, although this is true, but God will bring them in the coming glory of our LORD, by means of the Man who died for them. The activity of His power in raising them from among the dead is secured by His passive and active work on the cross and in resurrection. The facts of Christ's death and resurrection secure a place "with Him" in His glory. His death for us is God's guarantee that we shall be with Him. His resurrection is the pledge of the resurrection of the sleeping ones. His act of power in raising the saints from the dead will surely make the reunion of the sleeping and the living an absolute fact. "Caught up together" to meet Him, and thus to be forever "with the LORD," are secured in His word of promise, "them that sleep, by means of Jesus will God bring with Him." The two "with Hims" are identical. but what comes between them illustrates the "by means of Jesus," for His activity is demonstrated by the expressions, the "coming of the Lord," "the Lord Himself shall descend," "the dead in Christ" rising, and the being "caught up to meet the Lord in the air."

VI. A REPRESENTATIVE SCENE

"We made known unto you the power and coming of our Lord Jesus Christ, but were eye-witnesses of His majesty . . . when we were with Him in the holy mount" (II. Pet. i. 16-18). The transfiguration scene was a picture of Christ's coming and power. The two men who were transfigured with Christ were typical characters— Moses a type of those who will be raised from the dead, and Elijah a type of those who will be taken away without dying. The topic of the two glorified men with the glorified Christ was, "His decease which He should accomplish at Jerusalem" (Luke ix. 31). His "decease" was His exodus in death on the cross, and not without significance is it that the glory scene should be identified with His "decease," for His exodus in death means for us the entrance into the glory.

VII. A CLUSTER OF STARS

There are a number of star words which shine out in the firmament of God's prophetic word. Among the many are the following: "Appointed," "Place," "At Home," "Fashioned," "Eternal Life," "Incorruptibility," "Earnest," "Reward,"* and "Right."

"Appointed" to the glory of His fellowship: "God hath not appointed us to wrath, but to obtain salvation by our Lord Jesus Christ, who died for us, that whether we watch or sleep we should live together with Him (I. Thess. v. 9, 10). The word "appointed" means to set in a place, as when

---

*For the fourteen rewards to the believer, see my book *Discipler's Manual*, under the chapter heading "The Discipler's Reward," published by Kregel Publications.

a candle is *"put* under a bushel" (Matt. v. 15), as when a body is *"laid* in a tomb" (Mark vi. 29), as when wine is *"set forth"* before a company (John ii. 10), as when one is *"ordained"* for a given purpose (John xv. 16), and as when a person is *"set"* in an office (1. Cor. xii. 18, 28). The one thing to which God has not appointed His own is to wrath; the one blessing which He assures us we shall obtain is "salvation by our LORD Jesus Christ"; the one reason He gives for this is, because Christ "died for us"; the one pledge is all of grace, therefore it applies to all, whether they "watch or sleep"; and the one end He has in view is, "We shall live together with Him."

"Place" in the glory of His Father's mansions. Christ's word of promise is, "I go to prepare a *place* for you, and if I go and prepare a *place* for you, I will come again and receive you to Myself" (John xiv. 2, 3). He has gone to prepare a place, but when He comes back He will not receive us to the place, but to Himself. It is not a cold place to which He brings us, but to His warm presence. A stately palace without the bridegroom would be a poor place for the bride's warm heart. The man she loves makes any place a palace. It is not without suggestion the way the word *"*place" occurs or its equivalent. There was *"no room"* for Him in the inn when He was born (Luke ii. 7), but there was a *"place"* called Calvary where they crucified Him (Luke xxiii. 33). The *"place* of a skull" (John xix. 17) was the place to which He went for us, and now as a result He has gone to "prepare a place" in the glory. The word *"bowed"* which is used to describe Christ's act in dying— "He *bowed* His head and gave up His spirit" (John xix. 30),—is rendered *"lay"* in describing His poverty, "The Son of Man hath not where to *lay* His head" (Matt. viii. 20). The only place He had to lay His head was on the

cross. He was placeless that He might place us. His place outside the camp has placed us inside the palace.

"At Home" in the glory of His presence. The words "at home" and "be present" in ii. Cor. v. 6, 8, 9, are the same. The Greek word means to be at home. As long as we are "at home" in the body we are absent from the LORD, but when we are absent from the body we shall be "at home with the LORD (R. V.). He was once at home in the presence of the glory of His Father's presence, but being commissioned by Him to come and put away sin by the sacrifice of Himself (Heb. ix. 26), He left the home of His glory, that He might bring us into the glory of His home. He states this in His comprehensive prayer in the Upper Room, where we find a sevenfold glory expressed.

1. The Father glorified by the Son—"Glorify Thy Son, that thy Son may also glorify Thee" (John xvii. 1). The glory of the Only Begotten was that He ever expressed the Brightness of God's glory, in all He was in His holiness.

2. The cross-expressed glory—"I have glorified Thee on the earth" (John xvii. 4). The work to which He consecrated Himself (ver. 19) was the work of redemption in dying for human guilt. The throne of God is illuminated by the light of Calvary.

3. The pre-incarnation glory—"The glory I had with Thee before the world was" (John xvii. 5). What that glory was we have some faint idea from Isaiah's vision (Is. vi.; John xii. 41).

4. The believer bringing glory to Christ—"I am glorified in them" (John xvii. 10). His glory is great in our salvation. To the name of Wilberforce a glory will ever be given because he was the emancipator of the slaves, but a higher glory is bestowed upon Him who has redeemed us to God by His blood.

5. The glory given to Christ—"The glory which Thou gavest Me" (John xvii. 22). That glory seems to be indicated by the oneness which Christ received for the redeemed in associating them with Himself and making them one with the Father as His children. He has a glory as the First-Begotten which He did not have as the Only-Begotten. As the head of a new race the Head is glorified by the race.

6. Christ's glory—"My glory" (John xvii. 24). Christ has a personal glory which is distinct from His acquired glory. The glory of His personal worth. Both His personal and acquired glory are objects of our admiration and worship.

7. Believers' glory with Christ—"The glory which Thou gavest Me I have given them" (John xvii. 22). As when a prince marries a poor maiden and gives her his name and position and thus lifts her out of her former position, so Christ in making us one with Himself has given us His name and position, but that position could never have been ours if He had not first come into our death and darkness. Believers when they fall asleep now are at home with the LORD, but in a larger sense they shall be at home when He comes for His own.

"Fashioned" like to His body of glory proclaims our correspondence to Him, for the word *"fashioned"* means like in form; that is, "to be *conformed* to the image of His Son (Phil. iii. 21; Rom. viii. 29). He was once made in the likeness of sinful flesh, yea, "made sin for us," and we are to be made like to Him, for when we shall see Him, we shall be like Him. "His name shall be in their foreheads," which means, He will look at us and see Himself. "I have just seen your fac-simile," said a friend one day to me, referring to my youngest son, whom he had just

passed in the street. The LORD shall see His complete
reproduction and resemblance in the redeemed upon whom
He shall look in the day of His glory. Men in the scientific
world talk a good deal about correspondence to type.
There shall be perfect correspondence to Christ by the
redeemed, for we shall not only be with Him, but like Him.

*"Eternal Life" in its fulness has its consummation in the
glory.* "When Christ who is our Life shall be manifested,
then shall we be manifested with Him in the glory (Col.
iii. 4, R. V.). Christ said the purpose of His first coming
was that we might have life, that life we should never have
had except He had died as the Corn of Wheat. The whole
chain of eternal life was forged in the fires of Calvary,
and now the cable is fastened to the anchor within the vail.
The strength and comprehensiveness of this may be gauged
by the following connecting links in the cable of grace.
The death of Christ is its *basis,* as to the ground of its
bestowment (John iii. 14, 15); the keeping of Christ is its
security, as to the certainty of its enjoyment (John x. 28);
the Word of God is its *assurance,* as to the validity of its
endowment (John v. 24; I. John v. 13); the Spirit of
Christ is its *power,* as to the strength of its empowerment
(John iv. 14); the love of God is its *evidence,* as to the
sphere of its environment (I. John iii. 15); the holiness
of God is its *reproduction,* as to the effect of its
accomplishment (Rom. vi. 22); faith in Christ is the
receiver, as to the partaking of its blessing (John iii. 16,
36; vi. 47); feeding upon Christ is its *secret,* as to the
means of its fellowship (John vi. 54); union with Christ
is the *explanation* of its meaning, as to knowing its nature
(John xvii. 3); Christ Himself is its *Embodiment,* as to
the fulness of its worth (I. John v. 20); God the Father is
its *Author,* as to the cause of its gift (Rom. vi. 22; I. John

v. 11), and the glory of God is its *consummation,* as to the place of its fulfilment (Jude 21).

"Incorruptibility" in a life of immortality is the character of the glory. The Gospel is threefold in its message. It is a *Gospel of grace* as expressed in the love of God in giving Christ for us (John iii. 16); it is a *Gospel of power,* as promised by Christ in the enduement of the Spirit, for holiness of heart and life and usefulness in service (Luke xxiv. 49; Acts i. 8); and it is a *Gospel of glory* (II. Cor. iv. 4, R.V.), opening up a vista of life and immortality, hence we find the Apostle Paul, in speaking of the Gospel, begins in the fifteenth chapter of First Corinthians by saying, "Christ died for our sins," and ends in declaring the "mortal shall put on immortality." Immortality proclaims a state of incorruptible bliss and holiness in an incorruptible body (I. Cor. xv. 54). Adam was not immortal, for if he had been he could never have fallen. Believers are not yet immortal. Christ is the only One who has immortality (I. Tim: vi. 16). Life and immortality have been brought to light through the gospel (II. Tim. i. 10), and these shall be known experimentally when our LORD returns; then this mortal shall put on immortality, and the corruptible shall be superseded by the incorruptible.

"Earnest." The Spirit as the Earnest is God's pledge of the glory. One of the seven "In whoms" of Ephesians is, "In Whom, ye were sealed with the Holy Spirit of promise, who is the Earnest of our inheritance, until the redemption of the purchased possession" (Eph. i. 13, 14). The purchase price of the final deliverance is the cross, and the Earnest of it is the Spirit. As the fruit which the spies brought from the land of Canaan was the pledge of what was there (Num. xiii. 23-26), so the Spirit is God's guarantee that we shall be in the glory, as He Himself

assures us by the Spirit—"He that hath wrought us for the selfsame thing is God who also hath given unto us the Earnest of the Spirit (ii. Cor. v. 5).

"Right." The right to the Tree of Life and the entry to the New Jerusalem is in the blood of Christ's atoning death. "Blessed are they that washed their robes, that they may have the right to come to the tree of life, and may enter in by the gates into the City" (Rev. xxii. 14, r.v.). The details of the glory of that city I have indicated in my little book "What Is Heaven?" Seiss, in the following quotation, gives an idea of its dimensions: "The Golden City for which the Church of the first-born is taught to look as its eternal home, is 1500 *miles square;* for 12,000 *stadia* make 1500 miles. John saw it measured, and this was the measure of it, just as wide as it is long, and just as high as it is wide; for the 'length and the breadth and the height of it are equal.' Here would be streets over streets, and stories over stories, up, up, up, to the height of 1500 miles, and each street 1500 miles long. Thus the city is a solid cube of golden constructions, 1500 miles every way. The base of it would stretch from furthest Maine to furthest Florida, and from the shore of the Atlantic to Colorado. It would cover all Britain, Ireland, France, Spain, Italy, Germany, Austria, Prussia, European Turkey and half of European Russia taken together. Great was the City of Nineveh, so great that Jonah had only *begun* to enter it after a day's journey. How long, then, would it take a man to explore this city of gold, whose every street is one-fifth the length of the diameter of the earth, and the number of whose main avenues, though a mile above each other, and a mile apart, would not be less than eight millions."

With such a Saviour for our possession, and with such
a prospect before us, it makes us cry out with saintly
Rutherford, "I have not a balance to weigh the worth of
my LORD Jesus. Heaven, ten heavens would not be the
beam of a balance to weigh Him in. Oh, if that Fair One
would take the mask off His fair face, that I might see
Him. A kiss of Him through His mask is half a heaven.
O day, dawn, O time, run fast, O Bridegroom, post, post
fast that we may meet! O heavens cleaye in two that that
bright face and head may set itself through the clouds."

Meantime till He comes—

> "Cling to the Crucified!
>   His death is life to thee—
>   Life for eternity.
>   His pains thy pardon seal;
>   His stripes thy bruises heal,
>   His cross proclaims thy peace,
>   Bids every sorrow cease.
>   His blood is all to thee,
>   It purges thee from sin
>   It sets thy spirit free,
>   It keeps the conscience clean.
> Cling to the Crucified!
>
> Cling to the Crucified!
>   His a heart of love,
>   Full as the hearts above;
>   Its depths of sympathy
>   Are all awake for thee;
>   His countenance is light,
>   Even to the darkest night.

That love shall never change—
    That light shall ne'er grow dim;
Charge thou thy faithless heart
    To find its all in Him.
Cling to the Crucified!"

13
Four Errors
Regarding the Atonement

The Christ of Calvary is the One who is walking in the midst of the people, and every error and evil is open to His eyes of fire. The trend of every new cult of modern teaching is to have no place for the atoning Saviour in the vicariousness of His death. Socialism can patronize Him and speak of Him for its own ends as the Pattern of Beneficence. Spiritualism can point to Him as a Great Medium to draw recruits under its own fell influence. New Thought can talk about Him as the Perfect Man, but stabs Him in the back by the denial of His substitutionary death. New Theology betrays Him by taking away the virtue of His once offered sacrifice for sin, in the self-evolved statement, that Christ is atoning in a continuous sense in the sufferings of all who are suffering in a so-called good cause. Christian Science repudiates the actuality of Christ's vicarious work by denying the reality of sin, and repudiating the actual humanity of our Lord. The fact is, every error of modern times, and ancient ones too, proves its evil and its wrong by the denial of the God-Man in the reality of His humanity, in the denial of the vitality of His Deity, and in the denial of His substitutionary death as an offering for sin.

There are four errors in relation to Christ's atonement which we do well to recognise and avoid. Some are preaching a Christ without a cross, others are preaching a cross without a Christ, others again are preaching the subjective side of the death of Christ and leaving out the objective side, and there are others who are preaching the objective side of the atonement and leaving out the subjective application of it.

A Crossless Christ, for me no refuge is,
A Christless Cross, to me no hope can bring,
The Christ and Cross, for me alone avail.

1.—*Some are preaching a Christ without a Cross.* A bloodless Gospel is no Gospel. A rock-bound coast is no harbour of refuge to the storm tossed mariner on a rudderless vessel who is being carried on to the cruel reef of rocks. What he needs is a life-boat. Unitarianism, New Thought, and The New Theology have no gleam of hope, no harbour of refuge in their so-called Gospel. On the outside of a Unitarian Chapel in the City of Edinburgh is this inscription, "There is one God, and one Mediator between God and men, the man, Christ Jesus." The omitted words are, "Who gave Himself a ransom for all" (I. Tim. ii. 5-6). To leave out the ransom is to stultify the mediatorial work of Christ, for it is by means of His ransom He mediates.

"The only Gospel I want is contained in the sermon on the Mount," said a minister to Dr. C. I. Scofield sometime ago. The doctor replied, "There is no gospel in the sermon on the Mount. There is not a single drop of blood there. The sermon on the Mount contains the maxims and morals of the King for His subjects, and not a salvation for the sinner." It goes without saying that the Gospel, in its practical outcome, inculcates and enjoins the morality and spirituality of the sermon on the Mount, but the sermon on the Mount does not embrace the Gospel of the Grace of God. One thing alone proves it, the sermon on the Mount says, "Forgive us our debts as we forgive our debtors," that makes forgiveness conditional upon our forgiving others. Whereas we are forgiven by means of the blood of Christ—"In Whom we have redemption, through His blood the forgiveness of sins, according to the riches of His grace" (Eph. i. 7); and when we are exhorted to forgive one another, it is on the ground of, and in like manner, as God's forgiveness to us—"Be ye kind one to another, tender-hearted, forgiving one another, even as God for Christ's sake hath forgiven us" (Eph. iv. 32). "According to the riches of God's grace," is the measure of God's forgiveness, and "for Christ's sake" is the ground of it, and not our forgiving others. We forgive others because we are forgiven, not to be forgiven.

"What do you think of New Thought?" asked an old lady of the writer, at the close of a Sunday morning service in the city of Brooklyn, "What do you think of it?" "Not much," was the reply. "Why did you ask me?" "Why, I went to hear a New Thought lecturer sometime ago, and at the close of the lecture I went and told the speaker I did not believe a word she had said." "What did she say?" "Why, she said, she supposed I believed in the vicarious work of Christ, but she did not believe the blood of one man could atone for the sins of many." "What would you have said to that?" "I agree with the New Thought lecturer," I replied, to the consternation of the old lady. "You do," she exclaimed. "My! You do surprise me. I should not have thought you would, after hearing you preach." "Let me explain," I replied, "I do not believe the blood of one *man* can atone for the sins of many, but you must remember that Christ is God as well as man. Paul said to the Elders of Ephesus 'Feed the Church of God which He hath purchased with His own blood.' The Church is called The Church of God, God's Church, and it has been purchased with '*His* blood,' that is, the blood of God. I don't understand the mystery of it, but I accept its revealed fact. Besides Paul says the same thing in his well-known words of faith, 'The Son of God who loved me, and gave Himself for me, namely, The Son, the God. 'The Son' in His relationship to the Father and the sons, and 'The God' as proclaiming His Diety. Therefore the One who died for us, is the Son of God, God the Son. That makes His death more than a man's, and since it is infinite in value it covers all who are finite and human."

There are four things we ever need to remember. First:—*Sin is an offence against God.* Every Spirit enlightened man confesses with David, "Against Thee, and Thee only, have I sinned, and done evil in Thy sight." Christ's death can only be explained in the light of this fact, namely. "He was delivered for our offences," otherwise His death is an outrage, a blunder, a meaningless farce, and an offence to reason. Sin explains the sacrifice of the Saviour, as one has said, "The cross is God's final treatment of sin, the one compendium work of grace, and the one hinge of human destiny. Apart from sin the cross has no meaning. It was the exhibition of the worst in the heart of man, and the best in the heart of God."

Second:—*God meets His own requirement in the death of Christ.* The one thing which distinguishes the gospel of God's grace and extinguishes the religions of the world, is, in the religions of the world the blood is flowing from the devotees to the gods to appease them, but with Christianity the blood is flowing from the God to the sinners.

> "See from His head, His hands, His feet,
>   Sorrow and love flow mingled down:
> Did e'er such love and sorrow meet,
>   Or thorns compose so rich a crown?"

God Himself meets His own requirement in the death of Christ. He is not acting apart from Him, therefore His action is God's act.

Third:—*The Gospel proclaims, Justice saves..* The Gospel declares God's righteousness as well as His mercy—"Whom God hath set forth to be a propitiation, through faith, in His blood, to declare His righteousness," (Rom. iii. 25, 26.) "There is no thought in propitiation of placating a vengeful God, but of doing right by His holy law, and so making it possible for Him righteously to show mercy." The Scotch woman rightly apprehended the truth, when in reply to Dr. Chalmers' question, as to what she was resting in for her soul's salvation, said, "I am resting in the justice of God."

Fourth:—*The vicarious death of Christ is the only work which brings satisfaction to the conscience.* Only that which satisfies God, can satisfy us. Dr. Chamberlain relates the experience of a Hindu devotee at Benares, who had dragged himself from a long distance to wash in the so-called sacred river Ganges. The devotee said, "If I can but reach the Ganges, the shame and

bondage and fear will be taken away." He reached the
Ganges and washed in its waters, but he got no relief.
He exclaimed, "The pain is still here, the pain is still
here," as he pressed his hand to his heart. Then he
heard the gospel, that "Christ died for our sins," and as
he listened with wondering ears and eyes, he said,
"That's what I want! That's what I want!" Christ
dying on our behalf is what meets our want and nothing
else does. Two men listening to a Unitarian lecturer on
Glasgow Green, who was speaking on Christ as a Model,
and depreciating Him as the Atoner of sin, listened for a
little while, then one said to the other, "Come awa'
Wullie, he's na' gude, his rape is no' long enough."
Christ in His death is the only One who reaches us.
There is something in the heart and conscience of man
which demands that sin shall be punished, and it is only
when we know that that demand is met, that rest of
conscience is obtained. The shekinah glory rested upon
the blood-sprinkled mercy-seat. Noah's dove rested only
in the Ark, as long as the judgment waters prevailed.
The Holy Ghost rested upon the Christ after He had
gone beneath the waters of Jordan, the symbol of His
greater baptism at the cross. We too only have rest
when we rest where God rests. We are rested when we
rest in His rest.

II. *Some are preaching the Cross without the Christ.*
The Romanist and Ritualist practically do this. I do not
mean that all Romanists and Ritualists do this, but they
make so much of the crucifix and ceremonies that
many obscure the living Christ. Perhaps there is no
incident better illustrates this, than the following. Some
years ago in Cornwall there was a ritualistic clergyman
of the Church of England, who was very religious and
zealous in Churchanity, but had not a saving knowledge
of Christ. Among other things, he contemplated building
a new steeple to the church building. He related to a
friend what he intended doing, whereupon the friend
startled him by asking, "Are you going to build the
steeple from the top? The friend knew he was putting

his religiosity in the place of the Redeemer. The clergyman saw his error, and discovered that he had no foundation for his faith, and that he was obscuring Christ by his ritual. The drapery of ritualism and the crucifix of a dead past will not avail. They hide the person of Christ and make His work of none effect. The statement of the wise man applies here. He said, "Whatsoever the Lord doeth it shall be for ever, nothing shall be put to it, nor anything taken from it." No one can enter into the rest of salvation so long as they do not rest on Christ's finished work. The Holy Spirit says, "For He that is entered into His rest, He also hath ceased from His own works as God did from His." (Heb. iv. 10). The undoubted reference is to Christ having finished His atoning work and His resting in consequence. Alford well says, "That a contrast is intended between the Jesus (Joshua), and the great High Priest who is gone through the heavens seems very plain. And if so, it would easily be accounted for, that Christ should be here introduced merely under the designation of "He that entereth into His rest." Alford further says : "The introduction of the words, ' He Himself also,' lifting out and dignifying the subject of the clause as compared with God, in a way which would hardly be done, had the assertion been merely of any man generally."

"Again, the Spirit says : He has "for ever sat down," that is, He will never rise up to open the question of sin again, for He has settled it once for all. Besides He on the Cross said, "It is finished," or more correctly "Accomplished." He filled to the full everything that was requisite, therefore all was fulfilled—filled full, and there is no room for man additions. Man's additions are man's assumptions.

It is strange how we often find those who are in some senses diameterically opposed to be in the same bed together. Thus the Ritualist and the Catholic Apostolic Evangelist both teach baptismal regeneration ; and now we have the ancient error of gnosticism reproduced in milleninal dawnism, for the co-existence of the eternal Sonship of the Christ, with the Christ of human existence, and the glorified Man at God's right hand, are denied. To quote from the modern apostle of ancient heresy, he says in referring to Christ's existence before He became man:

" Previous to that time He was a perfect spiritual being, and since His resurrection He is a perfect spiritual being of the highest or divine order. It was not until the time of His consecration, even unto death, as typified in His baptism, that He received the earnest of His inheritance of the divine nature. The human nature had to be consecrated to death before He could receive even the pledge of the divine nature. And not until that consecration was actually carried out, and He had actually sacrificed the human nature, even unto death, did our Lord become a full partaker of the divine nature."

There is the denial of three essential things in this statement. That Jesus was not divine before He became man ; that Christ was not divine while He was on earth, He was human only ; and that He is not human now but divine. This is practically to make three personalities. He was angelic before He became a man, by becoming a man He ceased to be angelic, and now He is neither angelic or human, but divine. One passage among the many to be found will refute such a mixed medley, and that is Phil. ii. 6-11. Notice the continuity of the same personality, and then look up the confirming scriptures:

  = Christ the Form of Deity.—" Being in the form of God." (Heb. i. 3).

  = Christ the Equality of Deity.—"Thought it not robbery to be equal with God. (John xiv. 9.)

  = Christ the Emptied of Glory.—" Made Himself of no reputation."—"emptied Himself."—(John xvii. 5).

  = Christ the Slave Becomer.—" Took upon Him the form of a servant " i.e. " slave." (John xiii. 4, 5.)

  = Christ the Identified with men.—" Made in the likeness of men." (Rom. viii. 3.)

  = Christ the Actual Man.—" Being found in fashion as a man." (I Tim. ii. 5).

  = Christ the Humble Servant.—" He humbled Himself." (I Peter ii. 21-24.)

= Christ the Obedient Son.—" Obedient unto death."
(John xvii. 4).

= Christ the Vicarious Sufferer.—" The death of the
cross." (Rom. iv. 25.)

= Christ the Exalted Man.—" God hath highly exalted
Him. (Acts ii. 33.)

There is no thought in this passage of Christ becoming someone else. He always was what He is, and ever will be what He is and was; but He assumed our nature that He might have the right to redeem by means of His death; and as our Representative He has become the Son of God in a sense in which He was not before, namely, as the First-Begotten from the dead, because as such He is bringing the many sons to the glory. There was a time when King George the 5th was only the Duke of York, then he became the Prince of Wales, and now he is King of England, but he is the same person although he has undergone a gradation of rank. So with Christ, He became in time what He was not in eternity, and He is now what He was not in the eternal past and the time past. He, the Eternal Son of God became the Son of Man and is the Son of God as representing the sons of God. Therefore, while Christ was perfectly human as man, He was perfectly Divine as God, and never was any other than He is and was in His personality. The Eternal Son of God gives value to His work in time, hence, it is a timeless work, which projects itself out in an eternal blessedness. This could never be if He were not Deity. Don't let us divorce what the Spirit has united in those pregnant and pointed words : " The Son of God, Who loved me and gave Himself for me." The work of the Cross tells out the worth of the Saviour, and the worth of the Saviour gives value to the work of the cross. The white light of His Deity is coloured by the ruddy glare of Calvary, but Calvary would have no light at all but for that white light. On the other hand the white light would only blind us, but for the Blood tint of the Cross, but now through the lens of Calvary it blesses us, and enables us with unveiled face to behold the glory of Jehovah.

III. *Some are preaching the subjective side of the Cross alone, and omitting the objective.* Some teachers on holiness entirely ignore the act of the Christ on the Cross, and speak not of it as a fact about an act, but call it "a process," hence, they mix up the fact of Christ's work with its result. As a factor the Atonement is a process in its practical outcome, but as a fact it is finished and complete. The exponent of the new theology in referring to a well-known infidel says of him, "His moral earnestness is a mark of his Christhood, and his work is a part of the atonement." Such a statement is blasphemous and a libel on the work of Christ. We are ready to admit because the Spirit emphasizes it, that the Atonement of Christ is the basis of all blessing, the inspiration of all true service, the igniter of all devoted missionary zeal, the mould of all holy living, the cause of all noble sacrifice, the soul of all whole-hearted consecration, the incentive to all unselfish generosity, and the mover to all loving help. But don't let us forget these are products not producers, the effects not the cause, the building not the foundation, the plant not the root, the fruit not the tree, the sunshine not the sun, the stream not the smitten rock. We must have the rock smitten before the stream flows, the sun before the sunshine, the tree before the fruit, the root before the plant, the foundation before the building, the cause before the effect, and the producer before the product.

A young girl, who applied for Church fellowship, unconsciously illustrated both the objective work of Christ in His Atonement on the Cross, and the subjective result of it, in the replies she gave to the writer in answer to the following question, "Why did Christ die?" She said, " I could not be saved in any other way."

" Can you give me a Scripture," I asked.

" Yes," Christ said, " The Son of Man must be lifted up."

" Can you give me another reason why Christ died?

" He died," was the reply, "That I might have eternal life."

" Scripture, please."

" John iii. 16, says : " For God so loved the world, that He gave His only begotten Son, that whosoever believeth in Him should not perish, but have everlasting life."

To draw out the faith of this lassie of eleven years still further, I said, " Can you give me another reason why Christ died ? "

" He died that I should not be wicked."

" Can you prove it from Scripture ? "

She replied, " I cannot remember a Scripture, but I know there are many."

I told her to turn up II Cor. v. 15, and she read, " He died for all, that they which live should not henceforth live unto themselves, but unto Him which died for them and rose again."

I thought I would try her yet once more, so I said, " Edith, could you give me yet one more reason why Christ died ? "

She thought a minute then she replied, " Yes, He died that I should not be of the world."

" Chapter and verse."

" I cannot remember one at the moment."

" Galatians i. 4, tells you."

She read, " Who gave Himself for our sins, that He might deliver us from this present evil world, according to the will of God and our Father."

Without knowing anything about objective and subjective she had apprehended the whole situation, for the first two scriptures which she gave speak of the objective work of Christ for us in securing salvation ; and in the two last scriptures she unconsciously demonstrated the subjective power of Christ's Atonement in its practical application.

In the Atonement of Christ we find a double blessing all the time. It is the foundation of faith's reliance and the flame of love's inspiration ; it is the cause of repentance's change and the conformer of the redeemed's consecration ; it is the basis of all blessing and the beautifier of all believers ; it is the means of the sinner's forgiveness and the mould of the saint's fervour, it is the remover of sin's guilt and the regulator of the servant's

work; it is the origin of hope's expectation and the passport to Heaven's Glory; and it is the death of every vice
and the incentive to every virtue. Cowper well says:

"THE CROSS!

There and there only . . . .
There and there only is the power to save.
There no delusive hope invites despair,
No mock'ry meets you, no deception there.
The spells and charms that blinded you before,
All vanish there and fascinate no more.

I am no preacher, let this hint suffice—
The Cross once seen, is death to every vice :
Else He that hung there suffered all His pain,
Bled, groaned, and agonised, and died in vain."

The Cross is not only the "death to every vice," but it
is the source of every virtue.

IV.—*Some are preaching the objective side of the Cross
of Christ's Atonement and omitting the subjective power
of it.* This is the fault often to be found in evangelism.
The root is the cause of the tree, but a tree which is all
root is only a stump; the scale is the basis of music, but
music which is all scale is wearisome; the foundation is the
base of the house, but the house which is all base is an
unfinished product; and the vine which is fruitless is only
fit for the fire. The above similes are ungrammatical and
impossible as illustrations of Christ's death, but they
express what is true in fact, when only the objective side
of Christ's work is presented. The Atonement of Christ
is always the adequate cause which produces an assimi-
lating consequence. In type, in illustration, and by explicit
statement the death of our Lord is the moulding power
as well as the meeting propitiation. As the blood protected
the Israelites on the night of the passover and also
separated them from the gods of Egypt, so the Paschal
Lamb saves from avenging justice and separates from sin's
unholy associations; as the blood of the offering cleansed
the leper and was also placed upon the different members

of the cleansed man's body, indicating he was consecrated to Jehovah henceforth; so the Blood of Christ not only cleanses the conscience from guilt, but it also claims the sinner as Christ's property.

Something of the balance of the truth may be apprehended, if the following contrastive alphabetical list of Scripture sentences are pondered. The death of Christ is the causative power which produces a corresponding action. The objective fact of Christ's Atonement is complete apart from us, and completes us in salvation; but that Atonement also produces consequences which mould and make as He, the Christ of Calvary imparts the spirit of Calvary into our life and labours.

Objective fact of Christ's Atonement	*Subjective factor of Christ's Atonement*
A. Atonement for sin—"Make reconciliation for the sins of the people" (Heb. ii. 17)	**A.** Associated with Christ's sufferings—" Fill up ... the afflictions of Christ." (Col. i. 24).
B. Bruised for sin—" Bruised for our iniquities" (Isaiah liii. 5).	**B.** Branded for Christ. — " I bear in my body the marks" (stigma) "of the Lord Jesus" (Gal. vi. 17)
C. Cursed for sin—" Made a curse for us" (Gal. iii. 13).	**C.** Conformed to Christ's death —"Made conformable to His death" (Phil. iii. 10).
D. Delivered on account of sin —"Delivered up on account of our offences" (Rom. iv. 25)	**D.** Dead to Sin—" Being dead to sin" (I Pet. ii. 24).
E. Endured the Cross—" Endured the Cross" (Heb. xii. 2).	**E.** Enduring for Christ—"Endure grief, suffering wrongfully .. Christ .. leaving us an example" (I Pet. ii. 19-21).
F. Finished the work—" It is finished" (John xix. 30).	**F.** Finishing the course—" I have finished my course." (II Tim. iv. 7).
G. Giving Himself — "Who loved me, and gave Himself for me" (Gal. ii. 20).	**G.** Giving ourselves.—" Gave their own selves to the Lord." (II Cor. viii. 5).
H. Healing—"Himself took our infirmities and bare our sicknesses" (Matt. viii. 17).	**H.** Healing—"By Whose stripes ye were healed." (I Pet. ii. 24)

I. Identification—"I am crucified with Christ"
(Gal. ii. 20).

J. Judgment—"God . . condemned sin in the flesh"
(Rom. viii. 3).

K. Kindness—"The kindness of God our Saviour, and His love toward man appeared"
(Titus iii. 4. R.V.)

L. Love—"Herein is love, not that we loved God, but that He loved us, and sent His Son to be the propitiation for our sins" (I John iv. 10).

M. Manifestation—"He was manifested to take away sins" (I John iii. 5).

N. Nearness—"Having therefore boldness to enter by the blood of Jesus . . . let us draw near" (Heb. x. 19-22).

O. Obedience—"Obedient unto death, even the death of the Cross" (Phil. ii. 8).

P. Purification—"When He had made purification" (atonement) "of sins, sat down" (Heb. i. 3 R.V.)

I. Identification—"They that are Christ's have crucified the flesh (Gal. v. 24).

J. Judgment -"We thus judge, that one died for all, therefore all died; and He died for all, that they which live should no longer live unto themselves, but unto Him Who died and rose again."
(II Cor. v. 14, 15 R.V.)

K. Kindness.—"Be ye kind one to another, tenderhearted, forgiving each other, even as God also in Christ forgave you. Be ye therefore imitators of God, as beloved children; and walk in love, even as Christ also loved you, and gave Himself up for us, an offering and a sacrifice to God for an odour of a sweet smell."
(Eph. iv. 32; v. 1, 2 R.V.)

L. Love.—"Hereby know we love, because He laid down His life for us; and we ought to lay down our lives for the brethren."
(I John iii. 16 R.V.)

M. Manifestation.—"The Son of God was manifested to destroy the works of the devil" (I John iii. 8).

N. Nearness—"Let us draw near . . . having our hearts sprinkled from an evil conscience." (Heb. x. 22).

O. Obedience—"Let this mind be in you, which was also in Christ Jesus" (Phil. ii. 5).

P. Purification.—"Who gave Himself for us, that He might redeem us from all iniquity, and purify unto Himself a people for His own possession."
(Titus ii. 14 R.V.)

Q. Quenchless love—"Many waters cannot quench love" (S.S. viii. 7). "The love of Christ" (Rom. viii. 35-39). "He loved me, and gave Himself for me"
(Gal. ii. 20).

R. Redemption—"In Whom we have redemption, through His blood" (Eph. i. 7).

S. Sanctification—"For their sakes I sanctify myself" (John xvii. 19).

T. Triumph—"Nailing it to His Cross; having spoiled principalities and powers .... triumphing over them in it" (Col. ii. 14, 15).

U. Union—"Numbered with the transgressors" (Isaiah liii. 12).

V. Vitalized—"Except a corn of wheat fall into the ground and die, it abideth alone: but if it die, it bringeth forth much fruit" (John xii. 24).

W. Work completed—"By one offering He hath perfected for ever them that are sanctified" (Heb. x. 14).

Z. Zeal—"The zeal of Thine house hath eaten me up, and the reproaches of them that reproached Thee are fallen upon me" (Ps. lxix. 9).

Q. Quenchless love—"We love Him because He first loved us." (I John iv. 19).

R. Redemption.—"Redeemed ... from your vain manner of life ... with precious blood ... of Christ." (I Pet. i. 18, 19 R.V.).

S. Santification. — "Sanctify the people with His own blood. (Heb. xiii. 12).

T. Triumph.—"Satan .. they overcame him by the blood of the Lamb, and by the word of their testimony." (Rev. xii. 9, 11).

U. Union. — "Baptized unto His death. (Rom. vi. 3, 4).

V. Vitalized.—"Except ye eat the flesh of the Son of Man, and drink His blood, ye have no life in you." (John vi. 53).

W. Work appreciated. — "As often as ye eat this bread and drink this cup, ye do shew the Lord's death till He come" (I Cor. xi. 26).

Z. Zeal.—"For even Christ pleased not Himself, but as it is written, the reproaches of them that reproached Thee fell on Me." (Rom. xv. 3).

MARSH BIBLE STUDY SERIES

EMBLEMS OF THE HOLY SPIRIT
Unique discussions of each of twelve figurative representations of the Spirit. This help and instruction will not only enlighten but will give joy and power in Christian living.

DISCIPLER'S MANUAL
This classic study covers the entire life and service of a believer considered as a Christian worker. These 34 concise studies begin with his assurance and end with his reward. Formerly *Fully Furnished.*

ILLUSTRATED BIBLE STUDY OUTLINES
Over 250 outlines of doctrinal and devotional themes are carefully expanded with verbal illustrations from Scripture and life. Beautiful seed thoughts for sermons, Bible study and class illustrations.

MAJOR BIBLE TRUTHS
This study book on the important laws of Biblical interpretation covers subjects of typology, the law of first mention, prophecy, names and titles of God and prayer. Formerly *Structural Principles of the Bible.*

1000 BIBLE STUDY OUTLINES
Prepare to share the Word of God with these nuggets of truth. Teach Bible doctrines with these expository and/or topical briefs.

DEVOTIONAL BIBLE STUDIES
Striking titles, appropriate texts, illustrative incidents, outline studies and helpful themes for personal Bible study and/or a teaching ministry. Formerly *Pearls, Points, and Parables.*

500 BIBLE STUDY OUTLINES
These rays of light from God's lamp of Truth will illumine Bible study. Suggestive and helpful thoughts, both devotionally and scholastically. Personal and practical aids.